Making Historical Costume Dolls

Jack Cassin-Scott

Making Historical
Costume Dolls

B. T. Batsford Ltd, London and Sydney

To my daughter Sabrina

First published 1975
© Jack Cassin-Scott 1975

ISBN 0 7134

Filmset by Keyspools Ltd, Golborne, Lancashire
Printed and bound in Great Britain by
William Clowes & Sons Ltd, London, Colchester and Beccles
for the publishers B. T. Batsford Ltd,
4 Fitzhardinge Street, London WIH OAH
and 23 Cross Street, Brookvale, NSW 2100 Australia

Contents

Acknowledgments

My thanks must go to my wife Marion for the preparation of the manuscript, and to my sister Eileen for making the costumes, also to my friend and colleague Mr Jack Blake for taking the photographs with such great patience.

Jack Cassin-Scott
London 1975

Introduction

Doll figures throughout the ages have always been a form of fascination for the human race, regarded no doubt as small replicas of themselves. They had been discovered in the most extraordinary places including tomb excavations many thousands of years old. Apart from being a fundamental play-thing they have taken their part in the industrial and economic life of countries. As fashion dolls or 'babies' as they were called, they were in vogue as early as the fourteenth century and gained great prominence in the late seventeenth and early eighteenth centuries. These were highly professionally made models created by the master doll- and costume-designers of their day, and were the forerunner of the later, drawn fashion plates which became possible through the early daguerreotype plates.

The early American colonists took with them their European mode of dress, the fashion dolls helping to keep alive the latest trends in dress, thus making the fashionable silhouette of the early and late nineteenth century the same in New York, London and Paris.

To those who choose to make these historical dolls the choice of designs are numerous: the Elizabethan era with its elaborate encrusted jewels and pearls of Spanish influence; also taken to America by the early Spanish settlers; the extravagant hooped skirts of the eighteenth century; the more demure elegance of Victoria's reign, all have their individual charming variations and contrasting fabrics. With modern modelling and casting materials, methods are now available to most amateurs to produce professional models.

I have tried to cut technicalities down to a minimum giving only the essential basic instructions. Making historical costume dolls needs a fair share of patience and practice, but the difficulties, if tackled with common sense and loving labour, can soon be overcome.

The early chapters explain the materials and tools required, and the simple detailed instructions on anatomy for modelling the head, arms and legs for both the male and the female models. The step-by-step stages are explained through the numerous illustrations. Simple pattern designs are included and fully explained. Difficult shapes have been avoided, thus allowing the beginner to start with confidence and encouragement. For each model there are painting and wig-making instructions, as well as patterns and an historical note on the costume.

Simple modelling instructions – material and tools required (Fig 1):

(*a*)   Plasticine: this is recommended as being the cleanest and easiest to handle material for our purpose. It is very pleasant to use and requires no damping with water like clay so therefore can be allowed to stand without any fear of breaking up or cracking.

(*b*)   A simple plain wooden modelling board with a small wooden dowel upright.

(*c*)   Modelling Tools: two wooden spatulas, one small, the other a medium sized spade type and a wire-ended modelling tool, also a pair of draughtsman's dividers.

(*d*)   Casting tools: A small flexible plastic bowl and jug, one packet of plaster of paris, a metal spatula for tidying up the plaster mould, a wooden kitchen spoon for stirring the water and plaster of paris.

Before we begin to model, we must practise to control our modelling material. Plasticine is known to most of us from childhood but we must familiarise ourselves again with its pliable properties. Take a piece and squeeze it into your hands, roll it out, knead it, until it becomes warm to the touch. Notice the fine detail that can be obtained when you push your fingers into it, and the lines from these become clearly imprinted on the surface. Make simple cylinder, cube and ball shapes. Gouge out with the wooden spatula or wire-ended modelling tool, eye sockets, mouth pieces, form lumps to represent noses and ears. Practise and practise until you feel confident that by following the simple shapes illustrated you can attempt to model the various parts required for your figure.

Like fashion designing, historical doll making is a stylized form of modelling. The figure must have grace and elegance regardless of the period. The height of the normal figure is on average seven-and-a-half heads tall. To give the model the desired style, the height should be increased to eight-and-a-half heads tall.

Techniques: Making the Figure

1

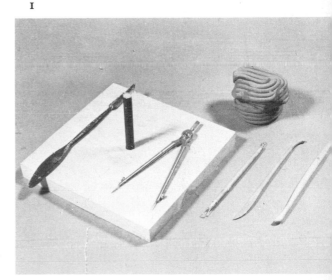

Now sketch out the following proportions before commencing the first stages of modelling. Providing the proportions are correct the sketch need only be of the roughest of pencilled outlines. To serve our purpose the following measurements are given as a general guide:

The Head: Make this in three equal proportions – (i) from the hair-line to the top of the eyebrows; (ii) from the eyebrows to the tip of the nose; (iii) from the tip of the nose to the base of the chin. From the centre of the mouth to the tip of the nose is the same distance as from the hair-line to the top of the head.

The Ears: These are approximately just below the brow-line to the base of the nose, the front of the ear being on the half-way mark between the front and back of the head.

The Eyes: These are half-way from the top of the head to the chin and are approximately set apart to the distance of one eye.

The Neck: This should be slightly longer than the normal and made about one-third the length of the head. For male models the neck should be modelled somewhat thicker than that of female models.

The Shoulders: These should be in breadth approximately just a little larger than the distance of the head and neck combined.

The lower chest and bosom line should be placed at a distance of approximately one-and-a-half times the breadth of the shoulders, from the crown of the head.

The lower part of the arms and hands should be approximately just over three hands long. The hand itself being at least half-a-head in length.

The Lower Leg and Knee: From the toes up to and including the knee should be about three hands long.

Further hints before commencing the modelling are: keep the features slightly longer than normal. Keep the eyes large and bring the corners of the eyes just slightly up and the eyebrows in a definite arch, the nose not so broad and the mouth not so full as that of a real person. The ears should be well-defined as a shape but not necessarily in detail. The neck should be elongated giving a long graceful swan-like effect.

The arms should be elongated, the fingers simplified length-ened and posed elegantly. The legs should be slim in the case of the female, long and graceful. The male leg should have a built up calf. The feet should be slightly lengthened to that of the normal.

With these proportions well established in the mind's eye, the work of modelling should now begin.

From the three basic shapes illustrated we will form the head and shoulders of our model. Onto the upright dowel core which is on the modelling board and should be of a sufficient size to accommodate the basic shapes, but a little shorter than the actual head and shoulders to be modelled, are placed first the larger block which forms the shoulders, then the cylinder shape, which is the neck, and finally the egg shape which is the head (Fig 2). First cutting both the egg and the cylinder shapes at the positions marked in Fig 3 at an angle of 45°. The neck piece should be placed central but slightly forward onto the shoulder block. Arching the back where the neck and the shoulder pieces meet, then round off the corners to form the shoulders. Place at the appropriate distance the chest or bosom with rolled pellets of plasticine. Mark with the small-ended tool a vertical line down the centre of the egg shape, then mark off with the dividers the brow line and with the tool draw a horizontal line (Fig 4). From this horizontal line place one plasticine pellet on either side and build outwards to form the forehead (Fig 5). Mark out the ear positions with the dividers, marking them with a pellet of plasticine. Now mark off the position where the nose would come, then the position of the chin, smooth the surplus of the chin into the neck. Now build up the cheek bones, remember-ing that the face is made from a bone and muscle construction. Blend the cheeks into the face. Add plasticine to form the mouth formation, smoothing this in but allowing the lip section to protrude a little further out than the cheeks. Now smooth these down so that the base of the cheeks blend into the corners of the mouth. The eyeballs are created with small round pellets of plasticine and placed into the correct position

2

3

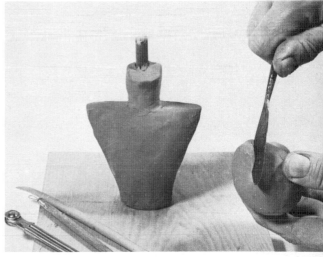

11

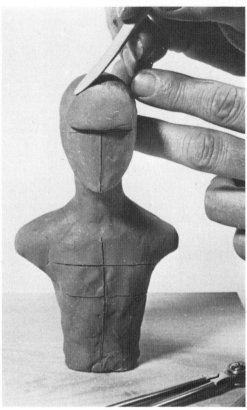

4

5

6

remembering that the distance between the eyes is the length of one eye. The upper eyelid is formed by beating out flat a tiny pellet of plasticine cut into a semi-circle then placed over the top of the eyeball and smoothed in, allowing just a slight protrusion over the eyeball itself. The nose-piece is now built on, starting just below the brow-line centre to form the bridge, then built out to form the fleshy protruding part. Finally model the ears. No great detail is required but they must be so made that they do not appear to be either too flat nor too protruding.

Always keep a round smoothness in your work and this should be observed when finishing off the neck, shoulders and chest line (Fig 6).

The modelling of the hand and fore-arm is made for both the left and right arms so two models must be made. This is simply done by using a thin dowel stick and at one end fasten five short lengths of 15 amp fuse wire bound securely with thread. This will act as the core. Now place on the plasticine rolling small pellets of plasticine in sausage shapes and placing these over the wire ends to form the fingers (Fig 7). Model these carefully then smooth them into the mass which will be the back and palm of the hand (Fig 8). Take special note of the joints and the boney sections such as the knuckles and clearly define the finger nails. Check with your own hands

7

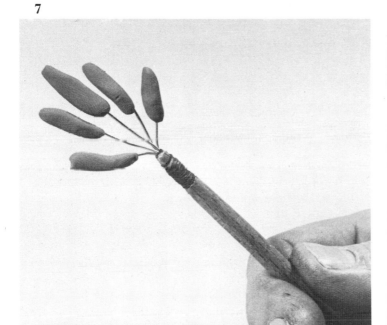

8

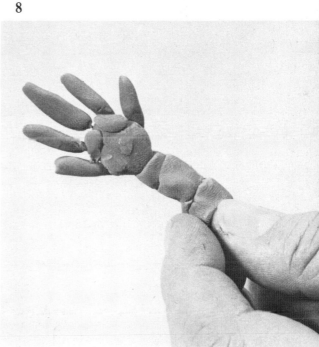

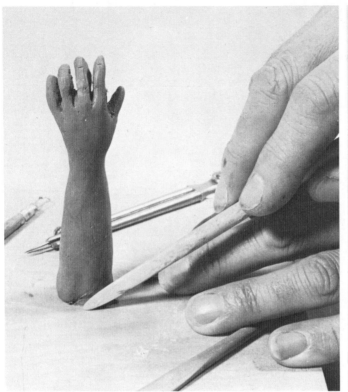

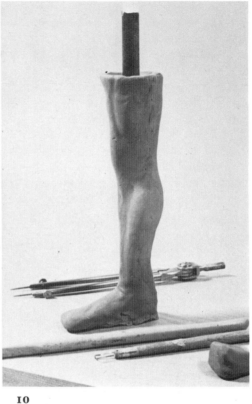

9

as you model. Now cover the dowel stick with plasticine and form into the fore-arm (Fig 9).

The lower leg section is somewhat easier although again two models must be made for the left and right legs. Again using a thin dowel stick as a core follow the curve line of the calf section making the male leg just that much more muscular, especially in the calf (Fig 10). Remember to make the feet just a little longer than normal, and, as they are covered in the final finished model, no detail is required. As with the head and shoulder section a nice rounding off of the modelling is essential. The casting is described in the next Chapter.

As the final assembled figure will stand approximately 40 cms. high, the following measurements should be followed closely, allowing for a final casting in a latex composition with a 10 per cent shrinkage. The head and shoulders should measure 10 cms., the arms, including the hands, 14 cms., and the legs, including the knee, 12 cms.

Making the plaster moulds

With the completion of the plasticine model to your satisfaction the next operation in making historical dolls can

Casting

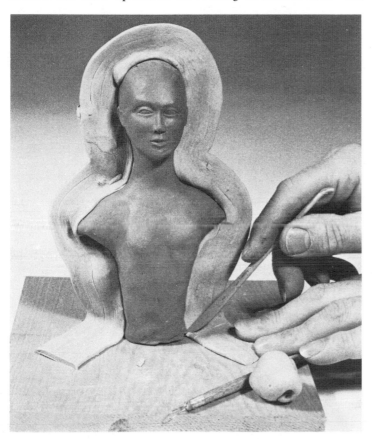

commence, that of making simple plaster-of-paris moulds. The torso and head, two legs, two arms will each be made in two-piece moulds. First we shall deal with the head and shoulder piece.

Roll out a length of plasticine with a small glass bottle making it about 1 cm. thick, and then it should be laid across the top of the head on the half-way divisional line dividing the model into a front and back part (Fig 11). Starting from the top of the head work down to just behind the ear, down the centre of the neck, across the shoulders and down to the wooden modelling board. Repeat down the other side. This strip is then built up to form a wall. This is then smoothed flat (Fig 12) and at evenly spaced intervals an indentation is pressed into the boundary wall. These are the registration keys for the other half of the mould when cast. Make a three-sided box of either strong board or thin metal sheeting, the edges of which are placed against the surrounding wall of plasticine (Fig 13). Rolls of plasticine are pressed into the sides joining them together. Around the base of the wall, strips of plasticine are placed to stop the liquid plaster from seeping out. The first half of our mould is ready to be made.

To do this we must make the plaster of paris mixture:

Fill the flexible plastic bowl with sufficient water to fill the cavity formed by box and model. Sprinkle the plaster of paris into the water until it settles just beneath the water level. Then begin to stir with the wooden spoon ensuring that there are no lumps left whatsoever in the mixture, and a creamy substance has resulted from the stirring. Then commence the pouring. Pour, not directly onto the plasticine model itself, but against the wall allowing the plaster to flow over the model. A slow continuous pour will help to expel most of the air surrounding the model. Fill the cavity up to the top and allow to set. The first half of the mould has now been made. Remove the screen and re-attach it (see Fig 14). Repeat the plaster-filling process, but do not forget to seal around the base of the screen with plasticine. With a soft paint brush cover the plaster face of the mould with a coat of ordinary household washing up liquid. This is to prevent the plaster adhering to the newly poured plaster of the other half. When this is dry repeat the plaster of paris procedure, as previously explained. When this is thoroughly dry the mould is gently prised apart and the original plasticine model is removed. This may be slightly damaged in the removal but its purpose has been served. Here the wire ended tool can be used with great care, any plasticine particles sticking to the plaster can be easily removed. The procedure for the hands and forearm, and fore-leg are exactly the same as for the head. The moulds when fairly dry, are now ready for the latex composition pouring.

Making the latex model

Each mould is reassembled and tied together with a strong elastic band and placed upside down so that the opening

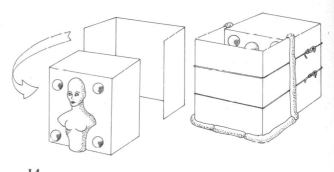

14

15

which now serves as a pour hole is uppermost, then the whole is tilted to an angle of 45°. This will facilitate the pouring (Fig 15). As the latex composition is cold, and in most cases comes from the manufacturers in a ready mixed state, nothing could be easier than to pour the required amount into a plastic jug for easier handling, and then to fill the moulds through their pour holes. After about ten minutes the latex composition residue is poured back into the jug. Left in the mould is a skin of latex composition which after being placed into any domestic oven at a temperature of between 50° and 70° for some 15 minutes, can be removed from the plaster mould (Figs 16 and 17). This skin is now transformed into a true reproduction of your modelled parts and after a further short period of exposure to a gentle heat can be cleaned of any 'flash' marks which may surround the joined areas, by a fine flour sandpaper. It is now ready for painting and assembling into the finished figure.

16

17

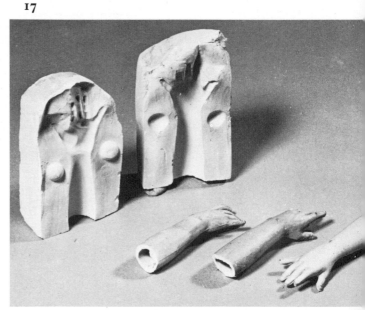

Making the Soft Bodies

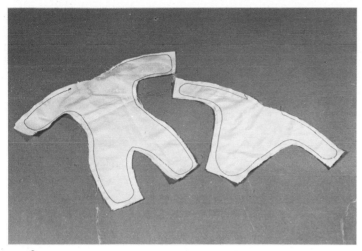

18

A soft body is made for each of the costume dolls so that each costume can be comfortably fitted and, if necessary, pinned and finally sewn on to. It is also possible to pinch in the waist to make a small wasp waist, or to pad out the hips just as each different costume or period requires it. This will give a more natural and individual appearance to the finished doll, making each one different. For the female figures there is naturally more padding for the hips and the waist is smaller than that for the male dolls. Although the basic shape of the body is the same, it can be altered by the amount and position of the stuffing used.

Where the costumes are long and full and fall to the ground, no legs are required on the model, so only a half-body is needed, as the dowel stick down the centre serves as the support.

To make a full body, cut out two pieces of strong material as shown in Fig 18. The colour of the material is of little importance as the body will eventually be hidden by the arms and clothes. Pin the two pieces of material together, then tack

so that when sewing together they will not slip about. Now either hand sew or machine together the pieces, starting at the centre neck, sewing along the shoulder, arm, and around either leg, and then up the other side to the neck, leaving about $2\frac{1}{2}$ cm. open to allow for turning inside out, and also for stuffing with the kapok.

To turn the body the right way out, it is best if the leg and arm extremities are first pushed through with the end of a pencil, this is to get a smooth, rounded shape at the ends. It is then very easy to turn the rest of the body out.

To stuff the body with kapok, push small quantities through the hole at the neck and push down to the extremities of the arms and legs first, again the end of a pencil is quite helpful in getting to these parts, then gradually fill the rest of the body. Make sure that the body is not too hard, but left firm and pliable, so that it can be pulled into any position required, and also drawn in at the waist-line, giving the female models a smaller waist. It is for this reason that the kapok is put in piece by piece.

When the body has been sufficiently stuffed, the neck edge should be sewn up to avoid the stuffing from coming out.

The half-body is made in a similar manner, but instead of having leg stumps, the pattern ends at the waist, but dips down slightly so as to give the body a more natural look.

The Display Stand

Requirements for the model display base:

1. One wooden base 18 cms. by 18 cms. by $2\frac{1}{2}$ cms.
2. Sufficient plastic fabric for covering the base, and a square of felt 18 cms. by 18 cms.
3. A length of dowel 38 cms. long
4. Two lengths of galvanised wire 55 cms. in length
5. One small hand drill
6. One small pair of long nosed pliers
7. One tube of rubber based adhesive
8. One sheet of fine sand-paper

Requirements for the soft body:

1. Plain pink material cut out from the body patterns. Material 60 cms. by 45 cms.
2. Kapok or other soft stuffing
3. Galvanised wire for the arms

The finished assembled figure will stand some 40 cms. in height which, I believe, is sufficient to make the creation of a costume look very effective.

To show the figure to advantage some sort of display stand is required, so what better than to incorporate such an item within the assembling instructions. There are two different assemblies, one for the female and the other for the male costume, although the male assembly can be used for either one as the illustrations show (Figs 20 and 21).

First, the simple assembling for the female model.

The display base of wood should be a square of 18 cms. by $2\frac{1}{2}$ cms. which should have a hole drilled through the centre to accommodate the long dowel stick. This is to support the upper body and arms only. The base is first covered with a plastic-type leather covering. The choice of colour is of little importance other than to choose either a neutral or contrasting colour to the costume. I prefer a neutral black finish. The dowel stick is then tapped gently into the centre hole of the base. This completed, the under side of the base is then covered with a square of felt underlay giving a professional finish to the display base stand.

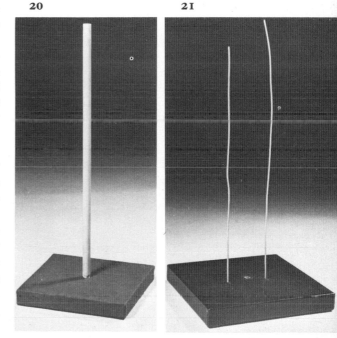

20   21

Painting
the Face

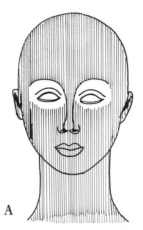

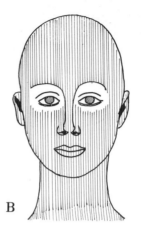

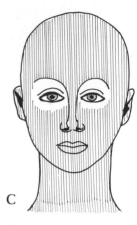

A   Paint the eye socket area in a bluish white.

B   A blue or brown spot for the iris, being careful that they are an equal distance from the nose and are the same size.

C   Mark in the pupil, correctly placed in the centre of the iris, cutting a line for the upper and lower eyelids, ensuring they are level.

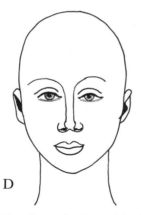

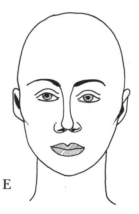

D   Cover the face with the flesh tone, bringing the tint to the outline of the eyes.

E and F   With a mixture of flesh tone and red paint in the cheeks and mouth. Darken the upper lip with a deeper tone of red. Mark in the eyebrows, nostrils and the separation line between the lips.

The Wig

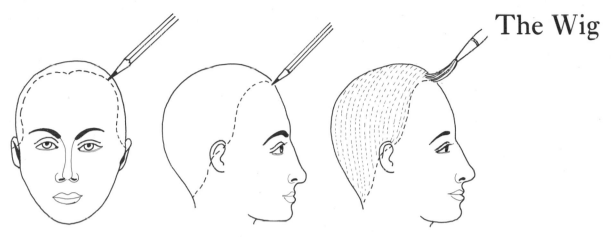

1 and 2   The head casting is marked with a fine pencil line across the hairline, then down either side to the nape of the neck.

3   The head part within the pencilled area is glued overall.

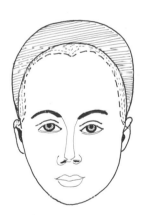

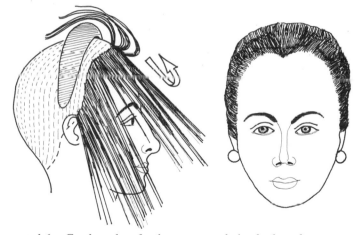

4   A roll of soft paper or a small piece of foam rubber cut to size is placed over the front of the head, just behind the hairline.

5 and 6   Cut lengths of nylon or crepe hair, the length being from the hairline to the back of the head – these are glued on to the hairline and then brought back over the paper roll and firmly pressed down.

23

Undergarments

Making the underskirt or petticoat

The petticoat can be made of a plain white cotton. It is made of a straight piece of material joined together at the back, and gathered at the top to fit the waist on a narrow band. The lower edge can be finished with a very narrow lace, but this is not necessary, as it is not really seen.

Drawers or underpants

Two pieces of white cotton material are cut out as in the diagram. Each separate piece is joined up the legs on the inside edge, and then the two pieces of material are joined together at the crutch to the waist at the back, and from the crutch just a little way up the front. The top is made to fit a waistband, the size of the waist of the model.

The bum roll

A bum roll is made by joining the two pieces of strong material together, leaving an opening to allow for turning the article inside out and then for stuffing with kapok. The opening can then be sewn together.

Projects

A Medieval Bishop

Requirements to make a medieval bishop figure:

1 A complete display base
2 Two lengths of wire supports
3 Castings of the leg
4 Two lengths of finger bandaging for the stockings
5 One pair of cut upper shoe shapes
6 One pair of cardboard soles
7 A length of wire for the arms
8 Male head casting
9 The costume
10 The hand castings
11 The costume accessories
12 The crook or crosier

The painting of the head and hands is as follows. No hair is required as the mitre cap is worn. The head and hands are painted overall in white priming. When dry paint the eye socket area with the priming white mixed with blue. Draw a small circle in the centre of the eyeball. This can be painted in either blue or white, this is the iris. In the centre of this coloured circle, taking the edges of the mouth as a guide with a fine paint brush, paint a black dot, this is the pupil. With a paint mixture of burnt sienna and white paint in the upper and lower eyelids. The upper lid is cut in with a slight arching line at the top of the iris. On the palette mix the following colours: white, burnt sienna and yellow until the desired tone of flesh is reached. Apply this tone to the face, bringing this colour up to and around the eyes, blending the eyelines gently with the flesh tone. Add to the already mixed flesh colour a small amount of burnt sienna, giving a somewhat deeper tinge of flesh colour, and this colour can now be painted around the eyes, down either side of the nose, under the bottom lip and under the chin. Blend this into the flesh colour. Add a light touch of red or pink under the cheekbone and blend it in, finishing the basic colouring of the face. Finally, with a pure burnt sienna colour mark in the eyebrows, the upper eyelids, following the same arching shape, the nostrils and the separation line between the lips. The hands are likewise painted in the flesh tones and in between the fingers blend in the deeper flesh tint and finally add a touch of red to indicate the knuckles and joints of the fingers.

Assembling the doll

Through the holes drilled in the completed display base insert the lengths of supporting wire. This being securely bent and fastened on the underside of the base with a staple. Then cover overall with a felt square base cloth. The leg castings are covered with the finger bandaging tube material secured both at the top and the bottom of the foot with glue. Cover with glue the front of the upper foot and the back of the cut out upper shoe shapes and press them firmly together. Glue the underside of the foot, the tabs of the upper shoe shape and the cardboard sole shapes. Press firmly together, by sticking the tabs down onto the foot and the soles firmly down. Drill a hole into the cardboard sole and push onto the wire. Make holes in all the extremities and centre neck of the stuffed soft body. Place a touch of glue on the leg stumps of the body and insert the wire through the leg openings and push firmly down to the top of the leg casting. A length of wire is pushed through the arm openings and the ends of the wires are turned over with the aid of the long nosed pliers. The head casting is glued on the inside and stuck firmly on to the shoulders of the stuffed soft body. The first garment to be placed over the head is the long ground length shirt type known as the alb, on which is sewn or stuck the orphrey ornamentation. Then comes the long scarf or stole which hangs from around the neck. Then is attached the amice which is placed behind the neck and shoulders and looks not unlike an embroidered collar-piece. Around the waist is tied a length of cord as the girdle. The soft body arm pieces are glued and the arm castings are placed over the wires and pushed up to the soft body and allowed to set. The mitre cap is fitted to the head and either glued or pinned securely. The cope is then fitted and the hands are placed in position to hold the pastoral staff or crosier.

24

No collection of period dolls would be complete without a religious figure being included. Throughout history religion played a great role in every day life. The ecclesiastical costume worn as illustrated changed very little since the twelfth century. The details of the garment are as follows. The alb, the long ground length gowned garment with long loose sleeves made of white linen, covered the nether-garment of the cassock. At the hem of the alb worn by Bishops was a band of embroidery known as the orphrey. The stole was a scarf-like strip of embroidered material which ended in a deep fringe and reached down just below the knee. The model being that of a Bishop, the stole hangs straight down. The amice was an oblong piece of material, usually of white linen, which was embroidered and called an 'apparel', and although it was tied on with tapes it fitted around the neck similar to an embroidered collar. The girdle, a long cord, which was tied round the waist, was made of a woven linen material, rope fashion. The cope was a ground length cape made from a complete semi-circle of velvet and various fine materials. It was fastened across the chest. The mitre hat was made of silk with pieces of decorated bands in front and at the back. The pastoral staff or crosier was made in the shape of a shepherds crook. It was made of various materials such as gold, silver, ivory or other material. It is carried in the left hand of the Bishop to allow him to bless the people with the right hand.

Costume

The making of the medieval bishop is quite simple. The alb, which is made of a white linen type of material, is cut out as shown in the diagram, and the two pieces joined together, leaving the neck open at the back so that it can be slipped over the model.

A small piece of ecclesiastical type of braiding or any type of small gold design trimming is required for either sticking or sewing to the base of the alb.

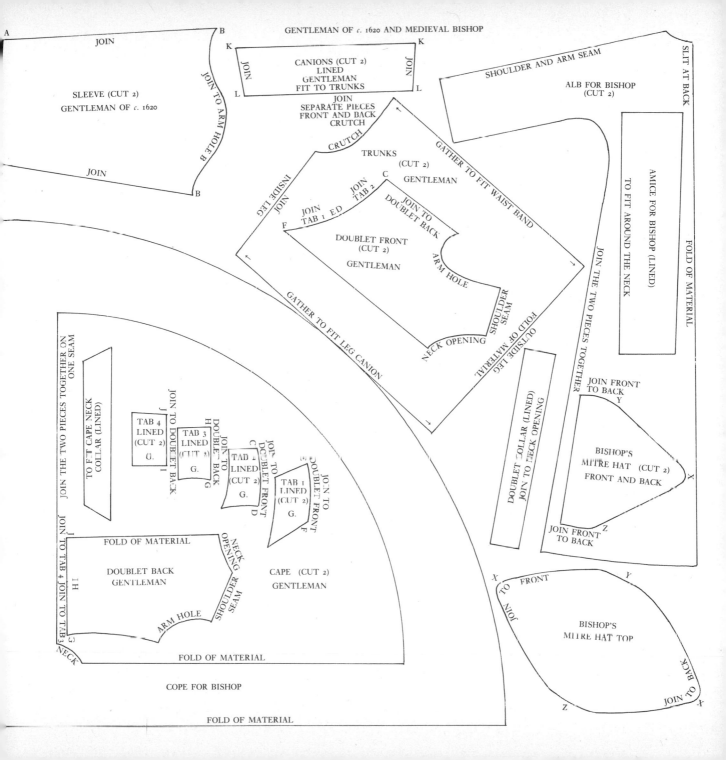

GENTLEMAN OF *c.* 1620 AND MEDIEVAL BISHOP

A

JOIN

B

SLEEVE (CUT 2)
GENTLEMAN OF *c.* 1620

JOIN

B

JOIN TO ARM HOLE B

K K

JOIN

CANIONS (CUT 2)
LINED
GENTLEMAN
FIT TO TRUNKS

JOIN

L L

JOIN
SEPARATE PIECES
FRONT AND BACK
CRUTCH

CRUTCH

TRUNKS
(CUT 2)
GENTLEMAN

INSIDE LEG

JOIN

JOIN
TAB 2

JOIN
TAB 1 ED

F

C

JOIN TO
DOUBLET BACK

DOUBLET FRONT
(CUT 2)

GENTLEMAN

ARM HOLE

SHOULDER SEAM

NECK OPENING

FOLD OF MATERIAL

GATHER TO FIT WAIST BAND

GATHER TO FIT LEG CANION

SHOULDER AND ARM SEAM

ALB FOR BISHOP
(CUT 2)

SLIT AT BACK

AMICE FOR BISHOP (LINED)

TO FIT AROUND THE NECK

FOLD OF MATERIAL

JOIN THE TWO PIECES TOGETHER

JOIN THE TWO PIECES TOGETHER ON ONE SEAM

TO FIT CAPE NECK COLLAR (LINED)

TAB 4
LINED
(CUT 2)
G.

J

I

JOIN TO DOUBLET BACK

TAB 3
LINED
(CUT 2)
G.

H

G

JOIN TO
DOUBLET BACK

TAB 2
LINED
(CUT 2)
G.

C

D

JOIN TO
DOUBLET FRONT

TAB 1
LINED
(CUT 2)
G.

E

F

JOIN TO
DOUBLET FRONT

OUTSIDE LEG

DOUBLET COLLAR (LINED)
JOIN TO NECK OPENING

JOIN FRONT
TO BACK

Y

BISHOP'S
MITRE HAT (CUT 2)
FRONT AND BACK

X

JOIN FRONT
TO BACK

Z

JOIN TO TAB 4 JOIN TO TAB 3

J

H

G

FOLD OF MATERIAL

DOUBLET BACK
GENTLEMAN

NECK OPENING

SHOULDER SEAM

ARM HOLE

NECK

CAPE (CUT 2)
GENTLEMAN

FOLD OF MATERIAL

COPE FOR BISHOP

FOLD OF MATERIAL

X

Y

JOIN TO FRONT

BISHOP'S
MITRE HAT TOP

Z

JOIN TO BACK

X

25

The collar, or amice, can be either a piece of material folded in half as in the diagram, or a wider piece of braid.

The girdle can be a length of white string or cord.

The cope, or ground length cape, is made as a complete semicircle of black velvet, lined in a red silky material.

The mitre hat, cut in three pieces as the diagram shows, has the two smaller pieces joined to the large piece which is the centre and folds up at the front and back, the straight pieces of the smaller parts being the part that fits over the head. Strips of thin braid are either sewn or stuck on to decorate the hat, as shown in the illustration.

26

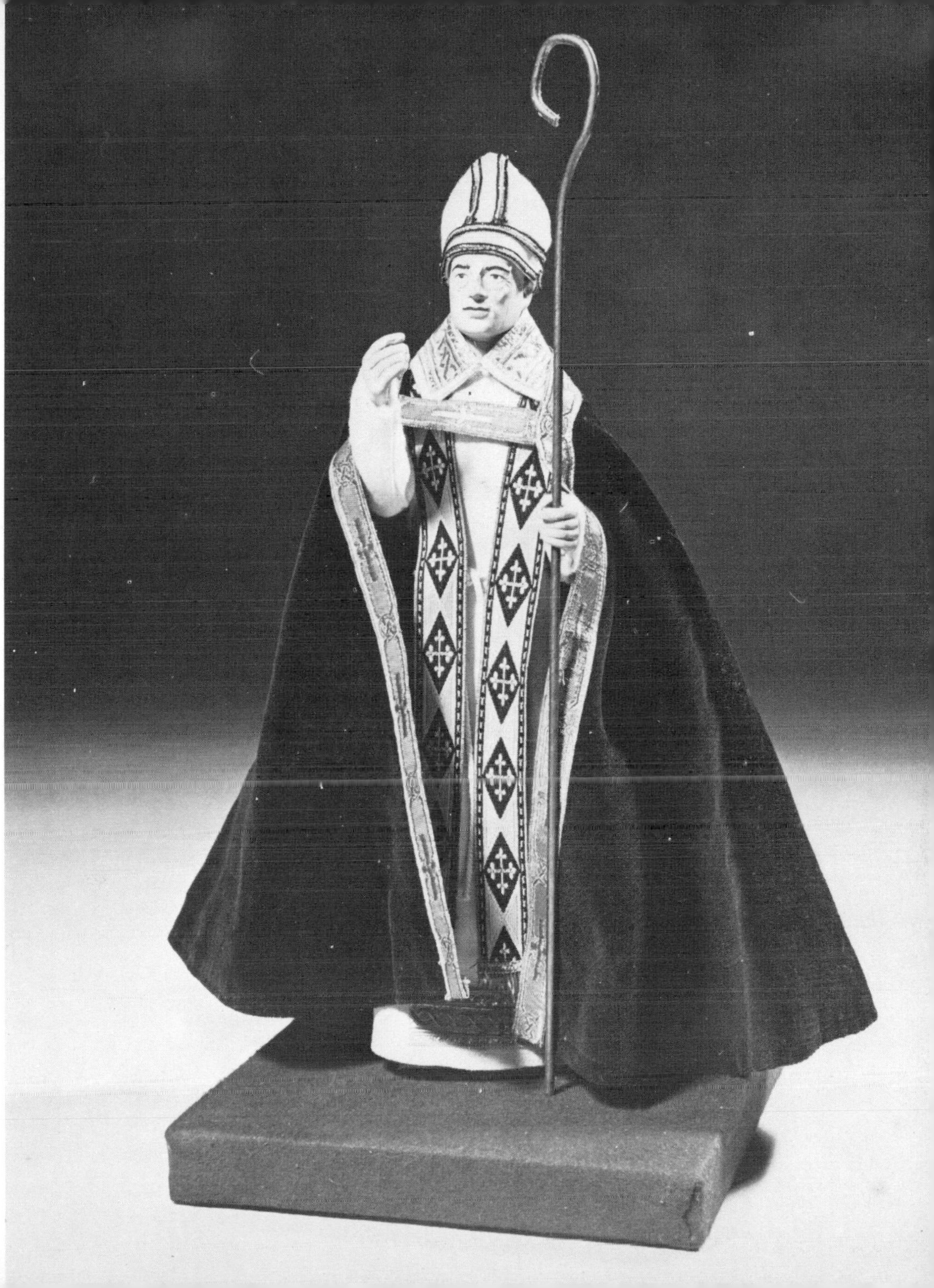

Medieval Lady of c. 1450

The necessary requirements for this very interesting doll figure are as follows:

1. A completed display stand
2. A dowel stick centre support
3. A stuffed half body
4. A length of wire for the arm support
5. Matt oil paints
6. Small length of crepe or nylon hair
7. Head and shoulder casting
8. The costume
9. Hand castings
10. The costume accessories

Having collected the necessary materials, the painting and assembling can begin. Paint the castings of the head and shoulders and hands with an overall priming of matt white and set aside to dry. Paint the eye socket area with a mixture of white and the slightest touch of blue. With either a deeper blue or brown paint in the iris on the eyeball. With a fine brush mark in with black the pupil of the eye taking the corners of the mouth as guide. With a mixture of white and burnt sienna on a fine brush mark out the upper and lower eyelids, curving the upper lid in a slightly arching line, just cutting the top of the blue or brown iris circle. With a mixture of white, yellow and burnt sienna make the flesh tone. Apply this to the head and shoulders and the hands. Bring the flesh tint up to the eyes blending carefully into the outline of the eye. With the flesh colour still in a wet stage, blend just under the cheek bone formation a mixture of red and white. Apply the same colour to the lips. The upper lip should be given a second application of a deeper tone of red. To bring out the formation of the face, apply a mixture of white and burnt sienna to the flesh colour and gently paint around the eyes, down either side of the nose, under the lower lip and finally under the chin. Having blended this into the face, set it aside to dry. Apply this colour down the outside of each finger and likewise set aside to dry. When thoroughly dry apply with a

pure burnt sienna colour the shape of the eyebrows, at this period it need only be a very fine line as they were shaven following the fashion of the day. Mark in the upper eyelid, the nostrils and the separation line between the lips. The fingers are likewise marked out with the same colour.

There is no hairstyle as such for this doll model, as the hair was completely covered with the exception of a twist or curled strand on the forehead which can be stuck on and the head and hands set aside ready to be assembled.

Assembling the doll

The dowel stick is fitted into the centre hole of the completed display base. The stuffed half body is nicked at the bottom and at the top centre and is then fitted over the dowel stick and pushed down until about $4\frac{1}{2}$ cm. of dowel stick is shown above the stuffed body. The extremities of the arms are pierced and a length of wire is pushed through the opening. When this is done, the ends of the protruding wire should be turned back on themselves to allow for easier dressing. The undergarment is now placed over the soft half body (Fig 27).

The head and shoulder piece is glued on the inside and pressed firmly over the dowel stick protrusion on to the soft body. The undergarment is pulled up over the shoulder casting and the bodice section fitted and neatly sewn up at the back. A spot of glue is placed either on the arm piece or the soft body arm pieces and these are brought together by inserting the arm and hand piece through the sleeve opening and firmly pushed together. The overgarment or houppelande is now fitted over and sewn up at the back (Fig 28). The hennin which is cut out in a thin card, a triangular shape, with the base the circumference of the head, is glued at the edges and formed into a cone shape. This in turn is covered with a piece of silk or decorated material. An oblong piece of silk or fine nylon is either placed over the hennin or suspended from the tip. The completed hat is now smeared with glue on the inside and pressed on to the head, exposing the lock of hair on the forehead and laying in a backward position. The frontlet, a

27

28

piece of embroidered material about 25 cm. long and 2 cm. wide is placed over the lower front of the hennin just above the forehead and tacked on. A wide length of gold braid is placed around the waist for the belt. The doll is then adjusted to the required position.

Historical note

This was an era when many changes in fashion were taking place, both in male and female clothes.

34

29

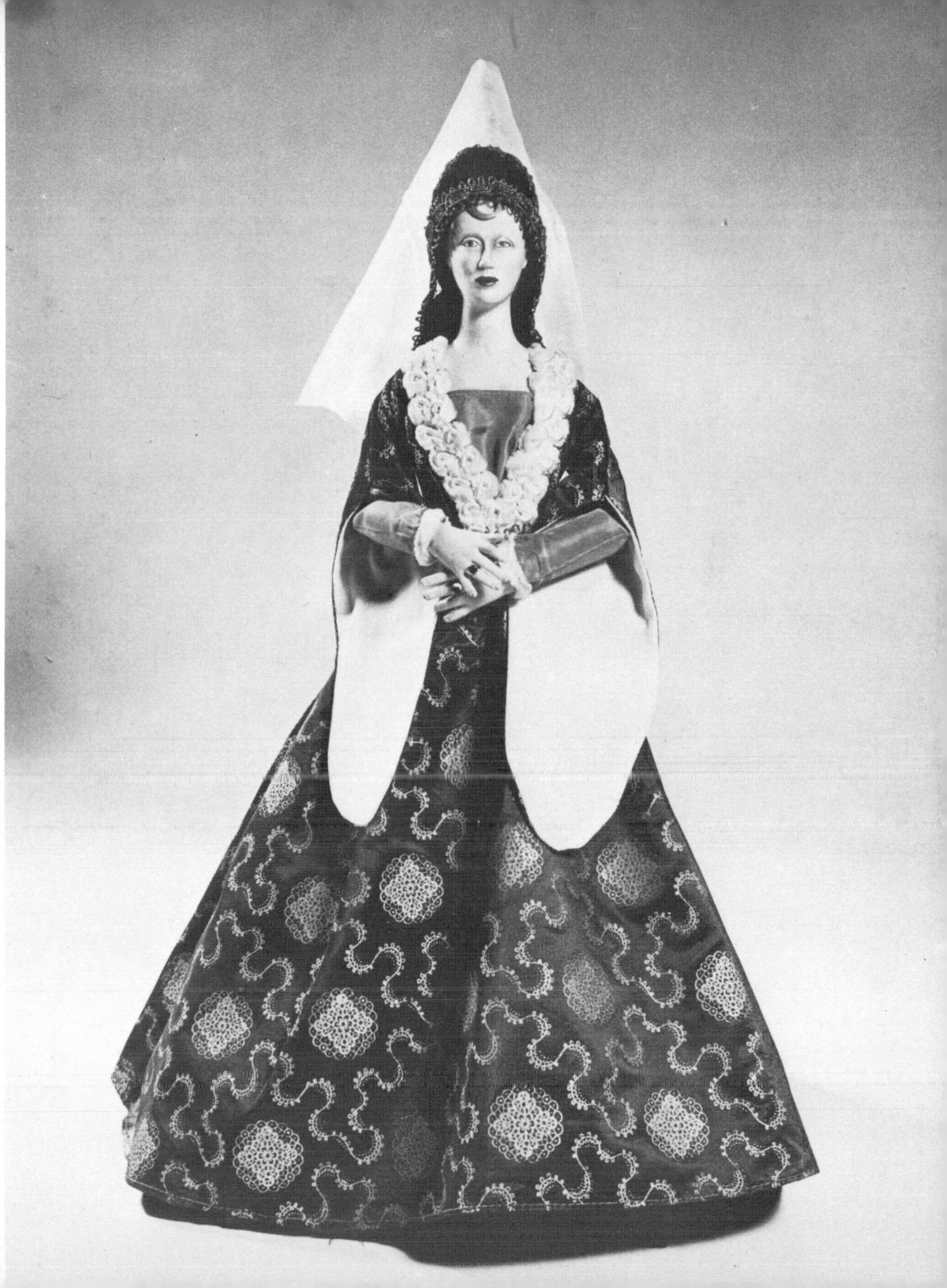

Women continued to wear the kirtle or underdress which fitted closely to the figure with tight sleeves fastening at the wrist, usually with many buttons. The sleeves from this underdress were visible through the large openings of the overgarment sleeves. By the second half of the fifteenth century the cote-hardie and the sideless surcoat had been superseded by the houppelande, which was an overgarment later known as the gown. The bodice, or upper part of the gown, fitted the figure fairly closely to the waist, some being closed and others open down the front to the waist. From the waist the gown fell into full long folds to the ground. There was a great variation in the sleeves, but many were funnel-shaped with large open cuffs reaching almost at the lower edge, to the ground. The materials in use had become richer, such as wool, silks, satins, taffetas, brocades, damask, lawn and gauze. Ornamentation was lavishly sewn or embroidered on to the clothes in the form of jewels and expensive fur trimmings. Belts, both plain and ornamented with jewels, were now worn around the waist instead of, as previously, around the hips.

The female headwear came in various fantastic forms. The popular and best known was the hennin which is attributed to the Flemish fashion. Flanders, being under the court of the Dukes of Burgundy, had adopted the fashion leadership from France which was otherwise occupied at this period in disastrous wars. Among others, both tall and short hennins were worn, the latter as shown in the illustration. This was covered with silk and decorated in braid, the frontlet being of cloth was likewise decorated and hung in streamers down either side of the face over the shoulders. Long veils of silk or transparent gauze either covered the hennin or were suspended from the upper point.

The fashionable ladies shaved their hair above the forehead and also their eyebrows. To accommodate the headgear, the hair was usually hidden and if it were visible it was just a curled strand on the forehead. Footwear was of soft leather, velvet or embroidered cloth.

Costume

An entire undergarment is made so that, if it is so desired, the overskirt can be held up to reveal it. The bodice front has a dart either side of the bust to give a better fit, and is then joined to the back pieces. After the shoulder seams have been sewn together, the sleeves can be set in, and the sides and sleeve seams joined. The underskirt is made in two parts joined at the sides and then gathered to fit the waist of the bodice.

The overdress has false overhanging sleeves which have to be lined and joined at the seams, as the join is at the shoulder edge of the bodice. The bodice has a very low front and is only joined just above the waistline. The edge around the neck is trimmed in a wide braid. When the bodice has been joined to the skirt, a gold braid can be used to encircle the waist as a belt.

When the overgarment has been put on, the sleeves of the undergarment are seen under the hanging sleeves, and the top of the bodice also shows under the deep overbodice.

For the headdress, a piece of material is cut out as in the diagram, as well as a piece of thin card slightly smaller, so that the material can be stuck to it and joined at the back. This makes the cone shape of the hennin, and over it is placed a net or very fine nylon, oblong in shape, to act as a veil. Over the front, slightly overlapping the forehead, there is a wide velvet ribbon edged each side with narrow gold trimming. This hangs down either side of the face.

Requirements for making and assembling an Elizabethan lady of the Court:

1. Completed display base with dowel stick support
2. Piece of cardboard 34 cms. long, bent to form a 22 cm. high cylindrical shape and a cut out cardboard circle to fit
3. A stuffed half body
4. A 32 cm. length of galvanised wire for the arms
5. Matt oil paints
6. Red nylon hair for wig
7. Head and shoulder casting
8. The costume
9. The hand castings
10. The costume accessories

Lady of the Elizabethan Era

This is the period of the farthingale, somewhat unnatural to our eyes but nonetheless the height of fashion at the Spanish, French and English Courts during the sixteenth century.

First the painting and wigging must be completed so that it will be dry for the final finished assembly. The technique of painting the face and hands and arranging the hair is as follows:

Prime the face, neck and shoulders, arms and hands in white. Allow this to dry. Give the eye socket areas a further coat of bluish white. Place a small circle in either blue or brown in the centre of the eyeball, then taking the corners of the mouth as a guide place a black dot in the centre of the coloured circle. Now with the burnt sienna and white mixture, mark out the upper and lower eyelids, arching the upper eyelid slightly. The face, neck and shoulders and hands are now painted overall in a very light shade of flesh tone, the mixture of white, yellow and burnt sienna being used. Before the face paint is dry add a little burnt sienna to some of the flesh tint and shade around the eyes, down either side of the nose, under the bottom lip and under the chin, carefully blending in the colour. With a pure burnt sienna colour line

30

in the nostrils now lightly mark out with burnt sienna mixed with a little red the arched eyebrows.

If you wish to follow the extreme fashion of that day you must first paint the face in matt white, and apply a bright red just under the cheek bones. It looks somewhat clownish but it was very fashionable. With the same red colour paint on the lips adding a somewhat darker red to the top lip. The lip separation is drawn with a fine line of burnt sienna.

Now the hair. Red or auburn-coloured nylon hair is used for the hair arrangements. Mark out with a fine pencil line high on the forehead, a peak in the centre front curving down to just above the ears. From this line cover the head with glue. Roll a small tube of soft paper and place it across the front from just above one ear to the other. This will act as the pad and wire frames. Cut pieces of nylon hair the length from the forehead to the back of the head. These are pressed onto the glued parts over the paper roll and firmly glued down at the back. This is continued over the whole area of the head. This method gives the impression of the hair style of that period. The hair can now be adorned with pearl beads. Earrings can be added by pinning or glueing a small pearl bead to either ear. The painting and wigging completed it is now set aside to dry.

Assembling the doll

Into the display base is tapped the dowel stick. The cylindrical shaped cardboard is joined at the edges with a length of sticky tape. The cut out circle, with a central cut out hole to fit over the dowel stick, is fitted to the top and likewise joined with sticky tape. Place the tube shape over the dowel. Make a slit in the soft half-body at centre top and centre bottom and slip it over the dowel stick (Fig 30). Make a very small nick at the extremities of both arm pieces and insert the length of wire, pushing through until lengths of wire protrude from each arm. With the long nosed pliers turn in the ends of the wire, this will facilitate the later fitting of the costume. Now smear the inside of the head piece with adhesive and gently

40

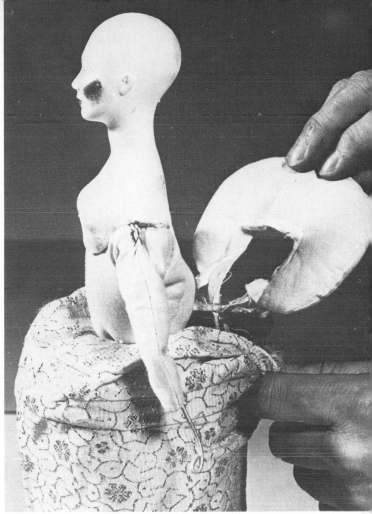

but firmly press it onto the soft half-body. Do the same for each arm, pushing them onto the protruding wires (Fig 31). The bum roll is fitted and tied around the waist with tapes (Fig 32). The assembled body is now ready for the costume.

If the simple pattern design is followed carefully no difficulty should be encountered. Most of the patterns are simple pieces, the diagrams are explained step-by-step in the making of the costume.

41

34

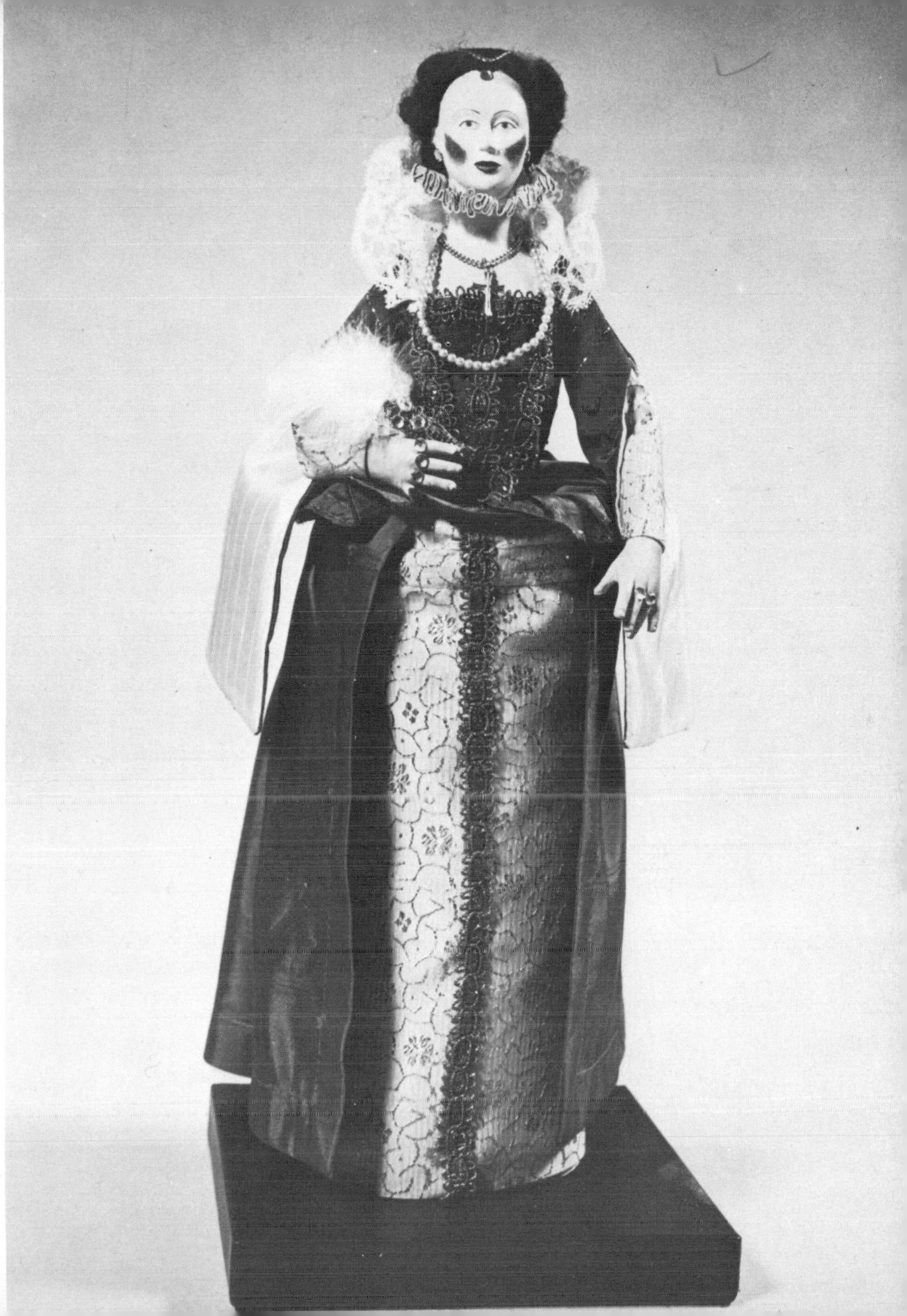

The dressing:
First the petticoat is fitted over the tube shape and sewn up at the waist. Over this is laid the overskirt, again being joined at the waist. The sleeves are slipped on over the wire pieces and the arms are inserted and stuck in. The bodice is fitted on and sewn up. Now remain only the final finishing touches such as fitting the ruff, jewelry and general accessories (Figs 33 and 34).

Historical note

The farthingale was an underskirt distended by circular hoops which ended in a wide circle at the feet. The farthingale skirt was gored so that it sloped stiffly outwards from the waist to the ground giving a very flat smooth surface. The fore-part or under petticoat was exposed through the triangular shaped front opening of the farthingale, the fore-part being usually embroidered, and contrasting with the skirt though often matching the sleeves. A padded roll was sometimes worn which looked somewhat like a life-belt, which was open at the front with tie-on tapes attached. It fitted around the hips and gave a slight tilt at the back and dip at the front. It was popularly known as 'the bum roll' and was not unlike the bustle of some 200 years later. The bodice was close fitting and rigid, sometimes stiffened with whalebone and long fronted, the waist was low and scollop-edged. The low neck style was formed by the upper border of a corset-like bodice being a low square, slightly arch shaped over the bosom décolletage in front. The fan shaped ruff worn with the long low-necked bodice was wired to stand up round the back of the head, rising from the edge and back of the décolletage spreading fan-wise behind the head. It was usually trimmed and edged with lace. This style was worn mainly by un-married ladies. The bodice sleeves which matched the fore-part were close fitting to the wrist and finished with hand ruffs. The hanging sleeves at this stage were sham, they matched the colour of the dress. A girdle was worn made of narrow ribbon, cord or chain. From the girdle articles such

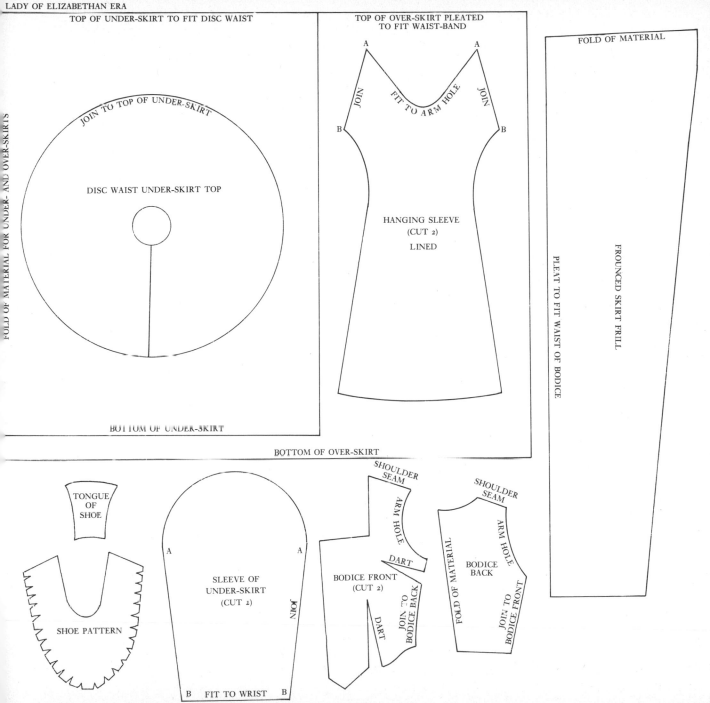

LADY OF ELIZABETHAN ERA

TOP OF UNDER-SKIRT TO FIT DISC WAIST

TOP OF OVER-SKIRT PLEATED
TO FIT WAIST-BAND

FOLD OF MATERIAL

FOLD OF MATERIAL FOR UNDER- AND OVER-SKIRTS

JOIN TO TOP OF UNDER-SKIRT

DISC WAIST UNDER-SKIRT TOP

A   A

JOIN   FIT TO ARM HOLE   JOIN

B   B

HANGING SLEEVE
(CUT 2)
LINED

FROUNCED SKIRT FRILL

PLEAT TO FIT WAIST OF BODICE

BOTTOM OF UNDER-SKIRT

BOTTOM OF OVER-SKIRT

TONGUE
OF
SHOE

SHOULDER
SEAM

SHOULDER
SEAM

A   A

ARM HOLE

ARM HOLE

FOLD OF MATERIAL

SLEEVE OF
UNDER-SKIRT
(CUT 1)

JOIN

DART

BODICE BACK

DART

JOIN TO
BODICE BACK

BODICE FRONT
(CUT 2)

SHOE PATTERN

B   FIT TO WRIST   B

JOIN TO
BODICE FRONT

as fans, muffs, mirrors or pomanders were suspended. The hair was fuzzed and crimped and built over pads and wire frames called 'Palisadoes' which came to a small widow's peak or dip in the centre and bunched out at the temples. Dyeing was very fashionable, saffron or red being the popular shades. Wigs and switches of false hair were often added to supplement any natural deficiency. Fans usually made from feathers radiated from a central decorative handle and were often carried. Large handkerchiefs made of lawn and trimmed with lace, others being embroidered and fringed or tasseled were carried. Stockings or hose which reached above or below the knee were either tailored or knitted. Pumps were worn by both male and female.

Costume

The Elizabethan lady wears an underskirt made of a straight piece of material, made into a tube shape, and joined to a circle of material, with a slit to fit over the waist.

It is not necessary to make a bodice for the undergarment, but a sleeve, fairly tight-fitting has to be made, as it can be seen under the hanging sleeve of the overdress.

The overskirt made in a slightly heavy kind of patterned damask, is again a straight piece of material, open at the front and pleated at the waist line to fit a waistband.

The bodice is cut out as shown in the diagram, the darts being sewn up first, and then the shoulder seams and side seams of the front and back. The hanging sleeves, which are lined in a contrasting material, after having been joined at the top only, are then set into the armholes with the sleeve seam uppermost, so that the hanging part falls from beneath.

The frounced frill is then pleated to fit the waist of the bodice and joined to it. The front of the bodice can then be decorated with any rich looking braid to cover the join down the front, and also across the top to make it look richer.

The collar is made of a lace scalloping, and the ruff of a narrower lace gathered around the neck.

A Gentleman
of *c.* 1610–1620

Requirements for making and assembling a gentleman of this period:

1 Completed display base with wire supports (see Fig 21)
2 Latex castings of lower limbs
3 Two lengths of finger bandaging tubes for the stockings
4 One pair of cut upper shoe shapes and two cardboard soles
5 A stuffed full body
6 A 32 cm. length of wire for the arms
7 A length of nylon or crepe hair for the wig and beard
8 The male head and shoulder casting
9 The costume
10 The hand castings
11 The costume accessories

With these requirements to hand the building up of the gentleman can begin. As with the Elizabethan lady, this was a period of extreme unnaturalness with a large amount of padding known as bombast. This fashion was popular throughout the whole of Europe and worn at the powerful Courts of Spain, France and England. The painting and wigging must be completed first so that it can be set aside to dry ready for the final assembly.

The painting technique for the hands and face of the gentleman are as follows:

The head casting is primed all over white. This is given time to dry. The eye socket area is given a further coat of paint, this time a slight blueish tinge is mixed with the priming white. As the paint is reasonably quick drying no great time is needed in applying the next operation, of placing a small circle of blue or brown in the centre of the eyeball itself. Now with a very fine brush place a small black dot to represent the pupil in the centre of the small circle. Taking the corners of the mouth as a guide as to its exact position again, with the fine brush this time loaded with a mixture of burnt sienna and white paint, mark out the upper and lower eyelids arching the upper eyelid just cutting the blue or brown circle. With a

47

paint mixture of white, yellow and burnt sienna, and as this is a male a little more burnt sienna is advisable. This is the flesh tone which is painted over all the face, neck and hands, bringing the flesh tone up to and around the eyes. Before the paint is dry add a little burnt sienna to the flesh colour and gently shade around the eyes, down either side of the nose, under the bottom lip and under the chin, and the ears. Blending this colour lightly into the mass flesh tone, mix a spot of red with white and brush just under the cheek-bone formation giving the face a ruddier look. With this same colour paint, paint in the mouth, then with a slightly deeper red, mark in the upper lip. When dry the lip separation is marked in with a fine line of pure burnt sienna. With the burnt sienna also, mark in the eyebrows, the upper eyelid and nostrils. The painting is now completed and allowed to dry.

The hair and beard: any colour of nylon or crepe hair can be used, the more natural looking the better as men wore their own hair at this period. Mark out with a fine pencil line the hair line on the forehead, down the sides and around the back of the ears onto the neck. Within this line cover the top and the back of the head with glue. Cut pieces of the hair the length from the forehead to the back of the head. Holding the length of the hair in the left hand place the leading edge onto the already glued hairline and with the left hand press firmly down. The hair should now be hanging forward over the face. Now take the hair and turn it back over itself to the back of the head and press gently but firmly onto the whole area of the head. With a small pair of sharp scissors, the hair can now be trimmed and shaped to the head itself and into the style required for this period. The face is now marked out faintly with the shape of the beard. This is lightly glued and small pieces of hair are laid on, each piece being firmly pressed down. When dry small scissors can be used to shape the beard style. The head is now completed and set aside ready for the final assembly.

Assembling the doll

Into the covered display stand are fitted the two lengths of wire set 5 cms. apart. These are placed through the drilled holes and the ends turned and fastened down with a staple. The bottom of the display stand is then covered with a square of felt. The lower leg castings are now covered with the stockings, these being pulled on and firmly glued down at the top. Cut off the correct length which covers the leg and the foot and glue the cut end firmly under the foot. Smear both the foot and the upper shoe pieces with glue, bringing them together and firmly pressing the shoe pieces onto the surface of the stockinged foot. The underside of the feet are now smeared with glue and the tabs on the shoe pieces are pressed down. The cardboard sole cut to the shape of each foot is glued into position. A hole is bored in through the underside of each foot and the legs are fitted over the wires.

The trunk hose with canions are now slipped over the wires and brought down to the legs and the canions fitted over the upper part of the covered leg castings to just below the knees. The stuffed body is nicked at the leg and arm extremities and also at the top centre. Through the leg and centre top opening is threaded the wire. A touch of glue on the ends of the stuffed body stumps will ensure that it will be held firm into the leg castings. The trunks are lightly stuffed with bombast to give it the correct fullness and the waist band is sewn onto the body. A length of wire is inserted into the arm pieces through the small openings, when this is completed the ends of the wire are bent over with the aid of the long nosed pliers thus avoiding any damage when fitting the doublet. The head and shoulder casting is glued on the inside and firmly pressed over the soft body and shoulders. This is allowed to set. Bend the arm wire pieces into a backward direction and slip on the doublet and bend the arms back to their normal position. The doublet is fastened down the front from the neck to the waist. A waist and sword belt is attached. The ruff is fitted framing the head. Arm pieces are now glued and fitted over the arm wire extremities up to the stumps of the soft body.

36

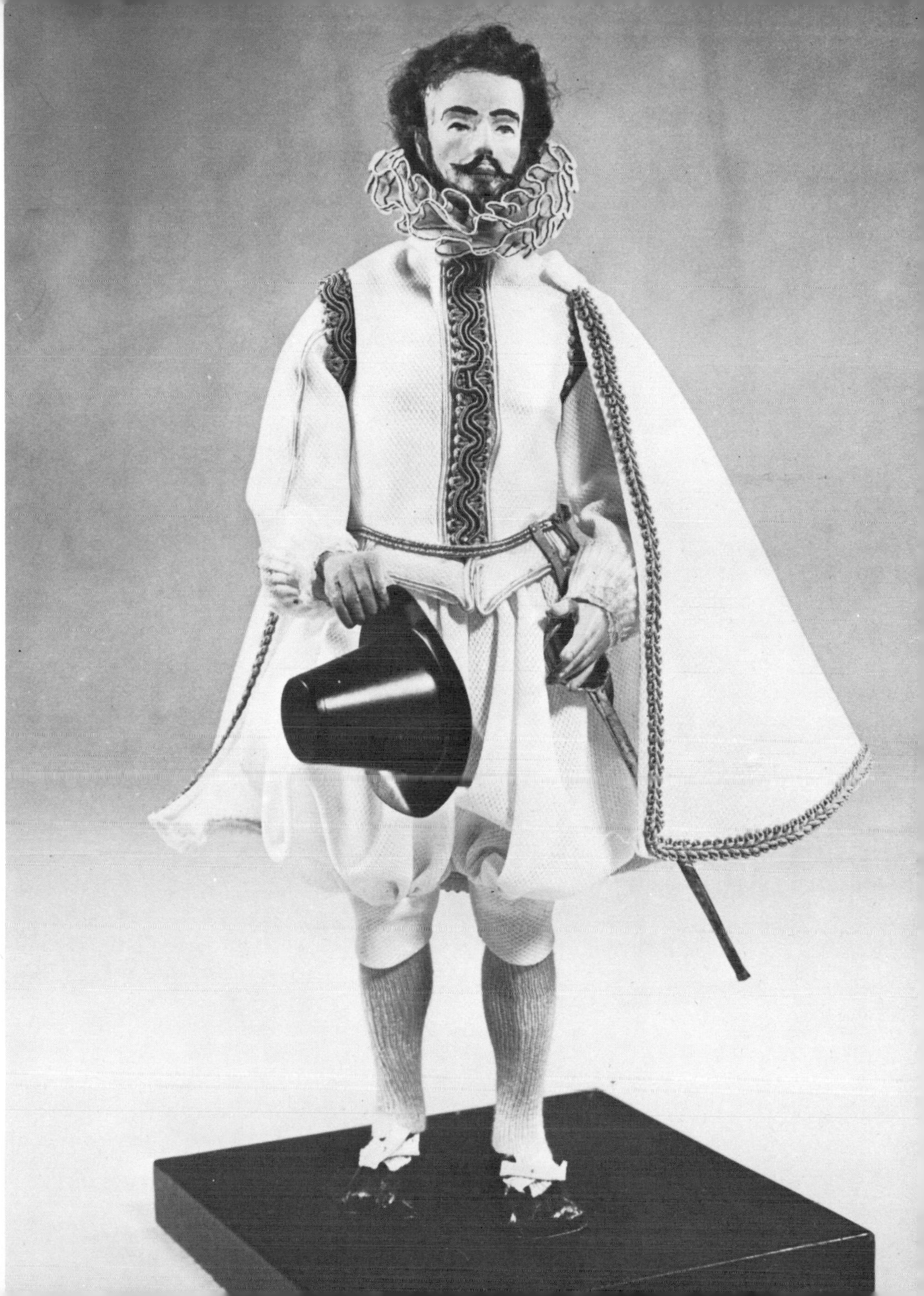

The lace cuffs are fitted over the wrists, the cape is attached and the final finishing touches are made with the general accessories.

Historical note

In this period the close fitting doublet acquired a more natural waist line position than the previous decade being busked with whalebone and stiffened with buckram. The short skirt of the doublet had a sharp dip in the front with square slightly over-lapping tabs. The plain closed sleeves were made from the same material and at the shoulders were wings that were projected welts which encircled the sleeve. A high standing collar which was stiffened with buckram was tied with band strings of ribbon which ended with a small tassel. The doublet was embroidered around the collar, down the front and down the sleeves from shoulder to wrist and around the short skirt tabs. Ruffs of all sizes were still worn and the cuffs were bordered with lace. The waist was usually encircled with a narrow belt fitted with hangers to carry a sword. This was sometimes replaced by a shoulder belt or baldric or sash. The trunk hose with canions were made very full and gathered closely at the waist falling to a wide base over the knees revealing the close fitting canions just below the knee. To give a very wide appearance, a curious fashion affectation, the trunks were lined with bombast of wool, flax, hair or cotton being used. On either side of the trunk hose were vertical slits which served the purpose of pockets. The stockings were either of knitted wool or silk and came in a variety of colours such as flesh, red, white, yellow and blue. The wearing of false carves was not unknown among the more fashionable male. Garters were in most cases very decorative apart from their use in securing stockings. Shoes were usually round at the toe and made of leather. The raised heel had now come into fashion and these were often made from cork. The tie-bows were hidden under large rosettes known as a rose. It was not uncommon to see a very fashionable dandy with his shoes almost completely covered by a rose. Large hats were very popular, and the men followed the habit of wearing them indoors for all formal events and always whilst eating. The cloak was very fashionable being made to match that of the doublet, the French cloak being the most popular style of this period which reached down to the knees.

Costume

See pattern on page 29 for this model.

A light, silky material is the most effective for this outfit. After having cut out the pieces as shown in the cutting diagram for the trunk hose, they are then joined on the inside of the legs, each piece separately. The two pieces are then joined together at the crutch to the waist. The canions can be lined in the same material or in a contrasting colour. These are then sewn to the bottom of the trunk hose which have been gathered to fit the calf of the leg. The top of the trunk hose is then gathered to fit around the waist of the model.

To make the doublet, the easiest way is to join the front and back parts at the shoulder seams and sew in the sleeves at the armhole opening. It is then very easy to sew together the sleeves and sides of the doublet. The four tabs are then sewn into their relative positions as shown in the diagram, and the collar can also be joined to the doublet at the neck edge.

To make the cape, which is a complete circle, it is probably necessary to cut two semi-circular shapes and join them together at the centre back. The collar can then be attached at the neck. If preferred the cape can be lined in the same or contrasting colour material.

Around the edge of the cape and down the front of the doublet can be stuck or sewn a contrasting narrow braid.

The ruff is made with a lace type of edging and gathered so that it gives the appearance of being fluted.

A Gentleman
of *c*. 1690

The requirements for this figure are listed below (Fig 37):

1 A completed display base
2 Two lengths of wire for the supports
3 Castings of the legs
4 Two lengths of finger bandaging tubes for the stockings
5 One pair of cut upper shoe shapes and tongue
6 A pair of cardboard soles
7 A stuffed full body
8 A 32 cm. length of wire for the arms
9 Nylon or crepe hair for making the wig
10 The male head and shoulder casting
11 The costume
12 The hand casts

The painting and wigging of the head and shoulders and the painting of the hand castings is as follows:

The head, shoulders and hands are first primed overall in a matt white. When this is dry a further matt coat of blueish white is painted over the eye socket area. A small circle in blue or brown is painted in the centre of the eyeball to make the iris of the eye. Then taking the corners of the mouth as a guide mark in a black dot in the centre of the coloured circle. This represents the pupil. With a mixture of burnt sienna and white paint with a very fine paint brush the upper eyelid just cutting the circle in a slightly arching line. Now mark in the lower eyeline. On the palette place the following colours: white, yellow and burnt sienna.

Mix these together and this will give you a flesh tint. With this colour paint the casting overall, special care must be taken with the face painting as the flesh tint should be brought up to the eyes very carefully. Before the paint is dry add a little more burnt sienna to the flesh tint and very lightly shade around the eyes and down either side of the nose, under the bottom lip and then under the chin. Blend this colour into the flesh colour already on the face. With a touch of red added to the flesh tone apply just under the cheek-bone and blend into the face. Paint the same colour onto the lips adding a

54

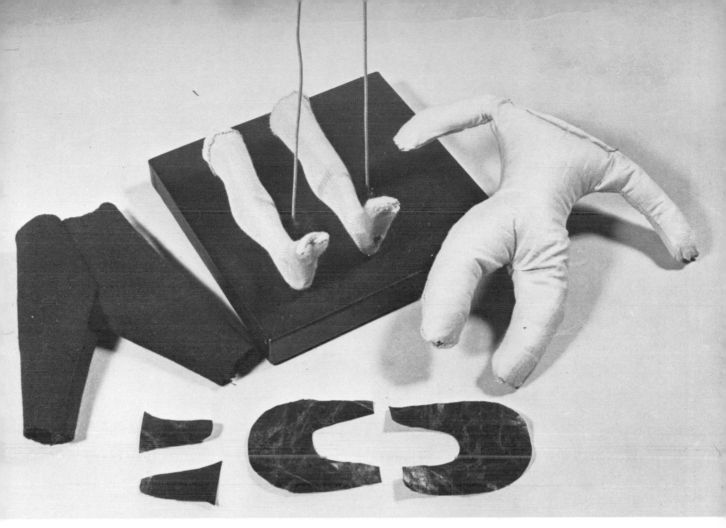

37

deeper tone of red to the upper lip. Set this aside to dry. Now
with a pure burnt sienna mark in the eyebrows, the upper eyelid, following the previous arching shape. Finally mark in
the nostrils and the separation line between the lips with the
same burnt sienna colour. The hands can now be painted
in between the fingers with the same colour as that used for
the nose and under the eyes. This is lightly blended in and
when dry can be marked out in a pure burnt sienna.

55

Making the wig

The hair-line is marked out along the top of the forehead and down either side of the face enclosing the ears, then continuing round to the back of the head to the nape of the neck. This then is smeared with glue. A length of hair is cut approximately 15 cms. × 5 cms. and holding it in the left hand lay it across the forehead and press it firmly down with the right hand along the hair line. The hair should now be hanging over the face. When the hair is firmly secured down on the hairline it should be turned back and pressed firmly onto the glued head and allowed to hang down the back. The same procedure should be followed on either side of the head covering the ears, then allowed to hang down the back. The three dangling ends are then taken together and turned back on themselves to form a loop and tied with a ribbon. Now cut off pieces of hair in various lengths and widths. Select one and glue both ends of each piece. Then take a paint brush handle and with a little application of glue, roll the hair around the handle very tightly, applying a little glue with each turn. Press firmly and slide off. Make about a dozen of these in various lengths then glue these into position on top and down the sides of the face, over the shoulders and round the back. Do not forget those on top of the head which form the horns. A light spray of hair lacquer will keep any loose hairs down. The head, complete with wig, may now be set aside and allowed to dry.

Assembling the doll

Into the covered display stand are fitted the two lengths of wire set approximately 5 cms. apart, as for the previous model. These are placed through the drill holes and the ends turned and fastened down with a staple. The bottom of the display stand is then covered with a square of felt. The lower leg castings are now covered with stockings. These being pulled on and firmly glued down at the feet only. Cut off the correct length which covers the whole leg and allow the top piece to remain open as these will be used to pull over the breeches on the finished assembled model. Smear both the foot and the upper shoes pieces with glue and bring them together and firmly press the shoe pieces onto the stockinged feet. Glue also the tongue piece which should be lined either with red leather or with red felt. This should be stuck on and allowed to stand up, being bent slightly forward. A small buckle completes the top of the footwear. The underside of the feet are now smeared with glue and the tabs on the shoe pieces are pressed down. The cardboard soles cut to the shape of each foot are glued into position. A hole is bored through the underside of each foot and the legs are fitted over the wires (Fig 38). The breeches are now slipped over (Fig 39), then the stuffed body glued at the leg stumps and placed over the wires and fitted into the breeches then sewn together at the waist. The stockings are now pulled well up and over the knees and a narrow ribbon tied around just under the knees and adorned with short ribbon pieces. The wire arm piece is fitted through

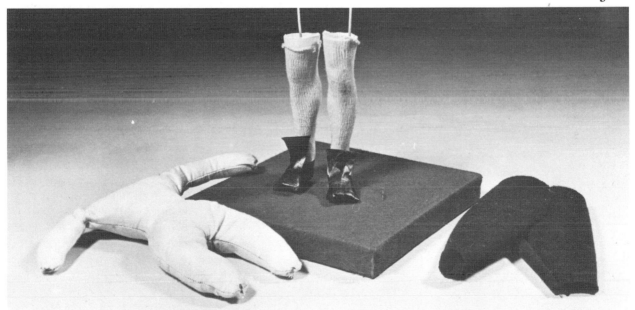

39   40

the arms and the head and shoulder casting glued and fitted over the stuffed body. The shirt front is placed on the chest and the neck band is fitted around the neck with a lace front. The coat is now fitted and fastened at the waist. The arm and hands castings are now placed into the sleeves and glued firmly in. The coat cuffs and the lace shirt frilled cuffs are fitted over the wrists and sewn on. Now take a strip of nylon fur material and glue one end to form a cylindrical shape to make the muff. Cut a length of ribbon approximately 15 cms.

long, tie it around the waist of the doll and then tie the end around the centre of the muff form letting the muff hang down from the waist. Form a sword shape from either metal or wood and attach it to a thin strip of leather thonging, fit it close to the pleat opening on the left hand side. Bend the right arm and place the hand into the muff opening, the left hand can be placed on the sword hilt or just allowed to be slightly forward, holding a handkerchief, hat or simply left empty. The figure is now complete.

Historical note

During this period a great change took place in men's attire. The coat which was now being made from cloth in place of silk had lengthened and the waistline became shaped and fitted with a slight flaring of the skirt. At the centre back the skirt was split up to the waist and decorated with buttons. Buttons and buttonholes being extremely popular were lavishly used on coats, cuffs and pockets. From the shoulders hung ornamentations of bunches of ribbons and loops. The coats were collarless and were worn either half-buttoned or fastened at the waist only. The breeches were plain and close fitting, they were knee length and usually black in colour. The neckwear of this period was either a lace cravat or the popular steinkerk which was a scarf-like piece of lawn loosely tied with the ends twisted and caught up through a button-hole ring. The stockings were pulled well up and over the breeches with a narrow garter being placed outside just below the knees, sometimes being ornamented with ribbon loops. The popular colour for men's shoes was black and they were square toed with red heels. The tongue which hung over the instep showed a red lining and the shoes were fastened either by ribbon bows or small buckles. The three-cornered hat became the male head-dress fashion of this period, being bound with gold or silver lace and sometimes trimmed with plumes or ribbons. Baldrics of embroidered silk or velvet or just plain leather belts were worn, from which usually hung the sword. Muffs were carried by gentlemen, these were attached by a ribbon belt from around the waist. This was a typically French fashion worn since the sixteenth century. The full bottom or French-style wigs had grown in size and had become even more artificial in appearance and were made in horsehair which retained the curls better. The wigs were parted in the centre and stood high over the forehead in two peaks like horns. The curls framed the face on either side of the parting, falling around the shoulders and down the back.

Costume

The breeches are made in two parts as the cutting diagram shows. Each part is joined at the leg seam first and then assembled by sewing together from the waist round the crutch and up again. To make them really tight-fitting a jersey type of material is recommended.

The shirt front is made of several rows of lace edging being sewn to a piece of material with a plain band at the top for the neck and a longer piece hanging down with a small bit of lace at the end. The bow can be made of a narrow piece of ribbon.

The coat is lined completely, apart from the sleeves. The two back halves of the coat are joined together to just beneath the waistline, allowing the rest to hang freely. After the shoulder seams have been sewn together, the sleeves can be set in and joined, as well as the sides of the coat to just below waist level.

The cuffs are a separate item and are also lined. They have two tucks to make them fit around the sleeves, and are just pinned at the wrist edge (B). The two pockets also have tucks and are sewn to the coat front just below the waistline. Very small studs are then attached down each side of the pockets, as well as a row down the right front of the coat to represent buttons, and also at the back down the split of the coat starting beneath the waist. For the buttonhole effect at the front and back, very short lengths of either russia braid or very narrow braid, cut to length is attached either by sticking or sewing opposite each button.

GENTLEMAN c. 1790 AND GENTLEMAN c. 1680

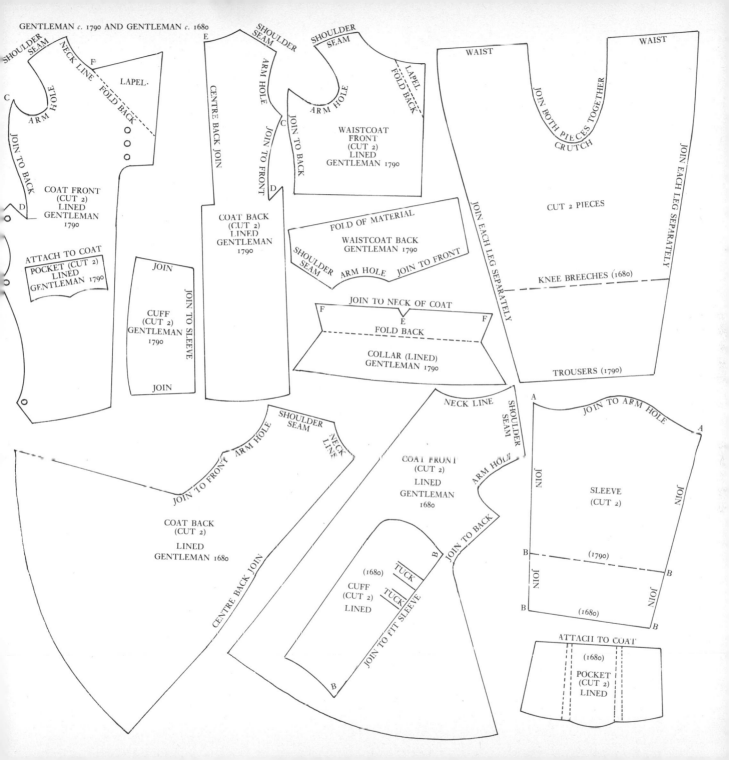

Lady in Crinoline
c. 1750

The following requirements are needed to make a lady of this period:

1. A completed display stand (see Fig 20)
2. A dowel stick centre support with a hole drilled through approximately a third of the way down
3. A length of wire to form the double panier
4. Pads, if required, to form the paniers
5. A stuffed half-body
6. A length of wire for the arm supports
7. The head and shoulder casting
8. Nylon or crepe hair for the wig
9. The arm and hand casting
10. The costume
11. The dress accessories

The painting of the head and shoulders and hands and the wigging is as follows:

The castings of the head and shoulders and hands are first primed overall in a matt white. When this is dry a further matt coat of blueish white is painted over the eye socket area. A small circle in blue or brown is painted in the centre of the eyeball to make the iris of the eye, then taking the corners of the mouth as a guide, mark in a black dot in the centre of the coloured circle. This represents the pupil. With a mixture of burnt sienna and white matt paint mark out with a very fine paint brush the upper eyelids just cutting the circle in a slightly arching line. Now mark in the lower eyeline. On the palette place the following colours: white, yellow and burnt sienna. Mix these together and as this is a female, more white should be added to give a delicate flesh tint. With this colour paint the castings overall. Special care must be taken with the face painting as the flesh tint should be brought up to the eyes very carefully. Before the paint is dry add a little more burnt sienna to the flesh tint and very lightly shade around the eyes, down either side of the nose, under the lower lip and chin. Blend this colour into the flesh colour already on the face. With a touch of red added to the flesh tone apply to just under

64

the cheek-bones and blend into the face. Place the same colour onto the lips adding a deeper red to the upper lip. Set this aside to dry. Now with a pure burnt sienna mark in the eyebrows, the upper eyelid following the previous arching shape. Finally, mark in the nostrils and the separation line between the lips with the same burnt sienna colour. The hands can now be painted in between the fingers with the same colour as that used for the nose and under the eyes. This is lightly blended in and when dry can be marked out in the pure burnt sienna.

The wig: the head-casting is now marked with a fine pencil line across the forehead at the hairline, then down either side, behind the ears and then round to the nape of the neck. The nylon or crepe hair is cut into three lengths, these being glued on either side of the head, the face now being com-area is now glued overall. The end of the first length of hair is now placed on the head at the hairline. The hair should now be hanging over the face. The other two lengths are likewise glued on either side of the head. The face now being completely covered. When this is dry and firmly held, the hair should be lifted up and turned on itself and glued down at the back. The side and back curls are made from lengths of hair which are glued at either end and then wrapped round the end of a small paint brush and firmly glued down. These when dry are then arranged at the sides and back of the main wig and firmly glued on. The hair should be of a light colour, blonde, white, light blue or mauve. A light coat of white paint can be applied to represent powdering if desired.

The painted casting should now be set aside until required for the final assembly.

Assembling the doll

Into the completed display base is tapped the dowel stick centre support. Measure about a third of the way down and bore a hole through the dowel then thread the wire forming a loop on one side, twisting the end around the stick and form the other loop. This forms the double panier structure. If the

65

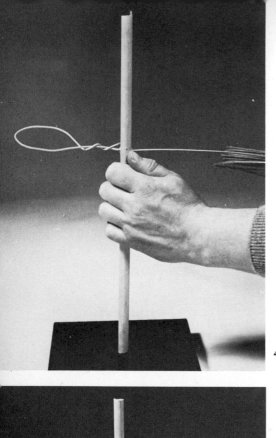

43

44

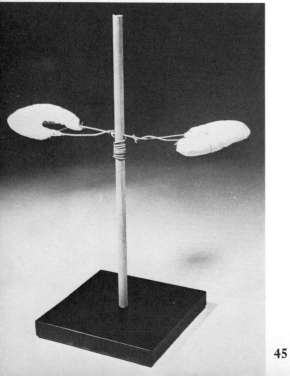

45

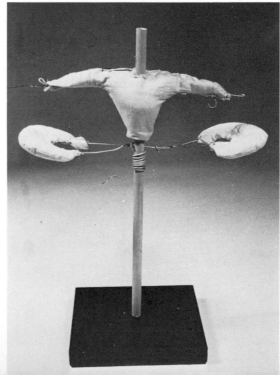

46

dress material is soft the bum roll forms can be attached to the wire loops to give a softer loop (Figs 43–45). Now slide over the soft half-body after nicking carefully the bottom, centre top and at either arm stump (Fig 46). The wire is inserted through the arm openings and the end bent over with the long-nosed pliers. The costume is placed over the completed structure and arranged over the panier wires. The head and shoulder casting is now glued onto the soft half-body and the dress bodice fitted over the upper structure (Fig 47). The bodice lace front is now placed in position and sewn on. The back is then pulled into the correct position and firmly sewn up. A touch of glue is applied to the soft half-body stumps and the arm and hand castings are now attached over the wire ends and then firmly onto the stumps themselves (Fig 48). The finishing touches such as necklaces and other accessories are arranged and the addition of a tall walking stick decorated with a ribboned bow completes the fashionable mode of the day of the crinoline lady of the 1750's. Simple and very effective. The arms can be placed in any position. Strike the most elegant pose then bend them into the required graceful position. Find a pose which shows the best points and features of the costume.

Historical note

The change in women's clothes was becoming more apparent during the middle of the eighteenth century. Dresses once more were being supported by frames of hoops known in this period as the oblong hoop and made in various materials such as whalebone, steel and cane. Due to their resemblance of basket work they were known under the French name of paniers. They made the dresses stand out in the shape of a bell. Although the walking in these dresses was somewhat difficult as their circumference were quite large, the fashion quickly spread to all classes. Although basically the same costume it had many variations and many names such as pocket panier dresses and elbow panier dresses. The front opening of this open robe was deep and was covered either by

67

47

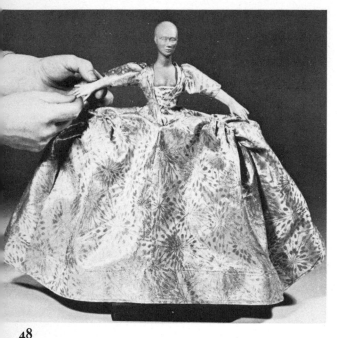

lace tuckers or corsage stomachers which was laced and ribboned. The half sleeves ended in ruffles of lace attached to the petticoat or undergarment. The back was in that of the sack dress often called the watteau style which consisted of two box pleats sewn down from the neck to the shoulders then allowed to fall into the fullness of the skirt. The hair styles were still at this period close to the head being brushed off the forehead with the back and sides dressed in curls. False hair pieces were often attached and the hair built up with cushion pads. An interesting note was the lavish use of scent at this time, a fashion which was quickly followed, and the carrying of perfume in various guises became the very popular fashion. Make up and face patches were also the mode of the day. The tall canes for all sexes were made from scented wood and decorated with ribbons and were held in the correct fashionable position, that being half way down.

Costume

The two bum rolls are made as previously described, one for each side loop of wire. The dress is made in a brocade type of material.

First the darts are sewn at the front and back of the bodice to give the waist a slightly flared-out appearance. After the sleeves have been gathered at the top to fit the armhole, and the front and back of the bodice have been joined at the shoulder seams, the sleeves can then be joined to the main part and the sides and sleeve seams sewn together. This is an easier way of setting in sleeves in such small models, as the more conventional way makes the sewing of such small armholes quite difficult.

After gathering the sides of the skirt where shown on the cutting diagram, the two pieces are then joined together, the front being one piece of material, a back panel is inserted. The waist is then gathered to fit the bottom of the bodice, and both parts joined together.

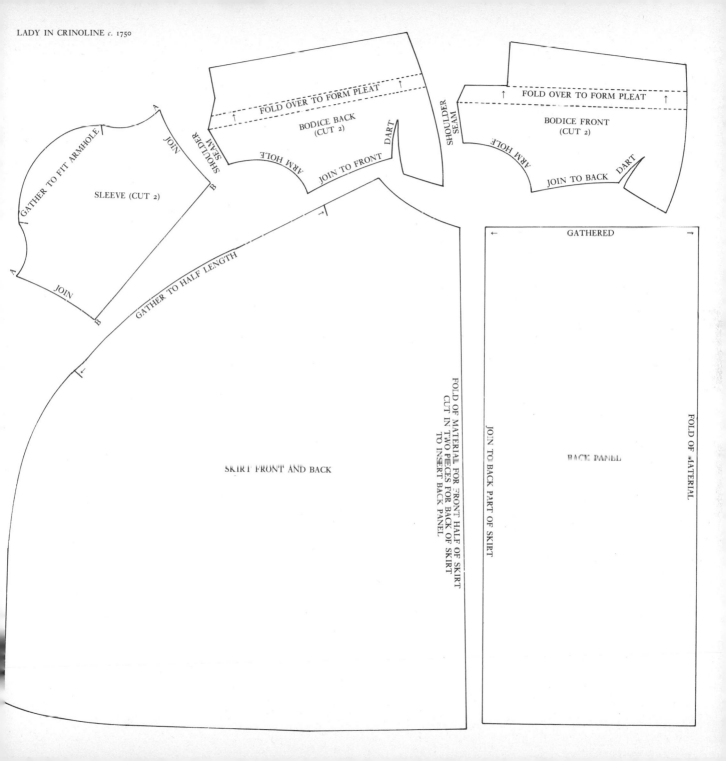

LADY IN CRINOLINE *c.* 1750

GATHER TO FIT ARMHOLE

SLEEVE (CUT 2)

JOIN

A

JOIN

B

A

B

JOIN

SHOULDER SEAM

FOLD OVER TO FORM PLEAT

BODICE BACK
(CUT 2)

ARM HOLE

JOIN TO FRONT

DART

SHOULDER SEAM

FOLD OVER TO FORM PLEAT

BODICE FRONT
(CUT 2)

ARM HOLE

JOIN TO BACK

DART

GATHER TO HALF LENGTH

SKIRT FRONT AND BACK

FOLD OF MATERIAL FOR FRONT HALF OF SKIRT
CUT IN TWO PIECES FOR BACK OF SKIRT
TO INSERT BACK PANEL

JOIN TO BACK PART OF SKIRT

GATHERED

BACK PANEL

FOLD OF MATERIAL

A Gentleman of *c*. 1790

The structural requirements for making this figure are as follows:

1. The completed display base (see Fig 21)
2. Two lengths of wire for the supports
3. The leg castings
4. Two short lengths of finger bandaging for the stockings
5. One pair of cut upper shoe shapes and a pair of cardboard soles
6. A stuffed full body
7. A length of wire for the arms
8. Nylon or crepe hair for making the wig
9. The male head and shoulder casting
10. The costume
11. The hand castings
12. The costume accessories

Painting the head and hands

The head and hands are given a primer of white matt undercoat paint. When dry, the eye socket area is given a further coat of blueish white. After a short wait the eyeball is marked with a circle and painted in with a blue or brown to represent the iris. When almost dry take a very fine brush and mark in with a small black dot, the pupil, taking the alignment of the corners of the mouth for their correct position. With a mixture of white and burnt sienna the upper and lower eyelids are marked in. The mixture of white, burnt sienna and yellow paint gives an excellent flesh tint. This can be varied by adding more of white or sienna to give the correct depth of the flesh colour required. This is now applied to the face and hands. Bring the flesh tone carefully up to the eyes. By adding more burnt sienna to the flesh tone and applying this colour around the eyes, down either side of the nose, under the lower lip and under the chin, carefully blend this into the face flesh tone. With the colour still wet, a touch of red should be placed just under the cheek-bone and blended in. With the same colour paint in the lips, darkening the top lip with a slightly deeper red. When this is dry, mark in with pure burnt sienna the eyebrows, the upper eyelid, the nostrils and the separation line between the lips. The head is now set aside to dry.

The hands are treated in much the same way. In between the fingers paint a mixture of the flesh tone and burnt sienna, blend this in. Add a touch of red to this colour and lightly paint across the knuckles and finger joints and blend in. Set this aside with the head to dry.

The wigging of this doll is very simple. Mark out with pencil the hairline, across the forehead, down the sides of the face, over the top and down the back of the ears to the nape of the neck. Smear this area with glue and then take a length of the hair and glue the ends, placing the leading edge onto the hairline centre allowing the hair to hang forward. Then repeat on either side. When the hair is firmly held along the hairline turn it back and over the head and firmly glue down at the nape of the neck. After firmly pressing down, set this aside to dry.

Assembling the doll

Dress the leg casting with a length of tube finger bandaging material, glueing the cut end firmly under the foot to make secure and glue the other end to the top of the leg casting. Smear the upper foot with glue. Likewise the cut upper shoe shape and firmly press both together smoothing them down and turning the edges underneath the foot. Glue the cardboard sole and press onto the foot casting. Fix the wire supports into the display base securely. Place the legs over the wire supports. The pantaloons are now pulled over the wires and onto the legs. Pierce the full stuffed body at each end of the arms and legs, then through the leg openings insert the wire ends and pull the body downwards. Glue the ends of the stumps and push firmly into the leg castings. Now pull the pantaloons up until the waistband reaches the waist of the stuffed body and sew firmly on (Fig 51). Thread a length of wire through the arm openings of the stuffed body and using the long nosed pliers turn the ends of the wire over. The complete head casting is smeared with glue on the inside and

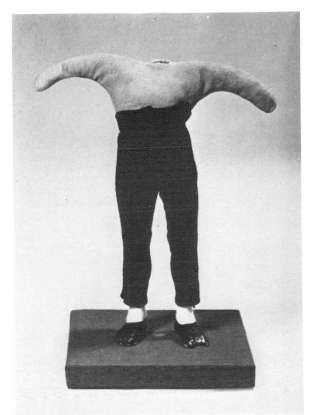

51

73

then pressed firmly onto the soft body. The shirt front and cravat are fitted around the throat and sewn onto the soft body front. The waistcoat is fitted on followed by the coat. The arms stumps of the stuffed body are glued and the arm castings are pushed into place over the wire supports. The doll is now ready to be fitted with the accessories and placed into a pose. Remember with the correct pose the costume can be shown off to its best advantage. With the doll supported only on the wires a few twists and turns will give it life and movement (Figs 52 and 53). Avoid extreme movement, get the feel of the position and pose in front of a mirror yourself in the correct attitudes required.

Historical note

This style followed the American and French Revolutions which brought great changes to existing ideas both in Governments and fashion. The male costume emerged in all its simplicity of cut. Gone too was the dress distinction of class with its fine embroideries and knee breeches or cullottes, the latter being replaced by pantaloons or trousers, the trousers being the symbol of the liberated or patriot bearing the French name of 'Sans Cullottes'. The coat had now become very much narrower in the back and the skirts were becoming just coat-tails. The stand-fall collar was high slightly cut back in front. The lapels were wide and turned back and over these were revealed lapels of the short double breasted square-cut waistcoat which had a stepped stand collar and wide blunt ended lapels. Also worn was an under-waistcoat which had become fashionable about this period, this had a shawl or roll collar which was usually made of some bright material which just showed above the turned back lapel of the over waistcoat. The other part of the under-waistcoat garment was usually in a dull coloured material of flannel, being made for warmth rather than decoration. They were called camisoles. The pantaloons were close fitting and shaped to the leg and ended at or just above the ankle, usually being buttoned up on the outer side up to the calf. A draw-string was sometimes attached to the bottom of the pantaloon and could be pulled around the ankle. Either heel-less slipper type shoes were worn with white stockings or boots of black leather and turn-downs of brown leather and boot straps at the sides. The three-cornered hat had disappeared and was replaced by the bicorne or tall small-brimmed hat. Walking sticks of various lengths were carried.

Costume

See pattern on page 61 for this model.

The breeches should be well-fitting, so the best kind of material to use is a jersey as this has a certain amount of stretch and can be made to fit closely. Two pieces of material are cut, the sides of each piece being joined together first to form the legs, which are joined together at the crutch to the waist.

The shirt front and cravat are made in a white material, such as linen; the front being a straight piece gathered in at the neck and the cravat a long, narrow piece of material with a piece of lace attached at the end for decoration, and fastened around the neck.

To make the waistcoat, the front parts have to be lined, so that the lapel can be turned back. The fronts are then joined at the shoulder and side seams to the back. When the waist-coat has been fitted on to the model, the front is fastened with two rows of large-headed pins, these give the impression of tiny buttons.

The coat is made up from several pieces of striped material, a silky finish is very effective. The collar is lined in the main material, and the rest of the coat is lined in a contrasting colour. The sleeves and cuffs do not need lining.

The back of the coat is joined together from the neckline to the waist, allowing the skirts to fall down separately. For buttons, small dog studs or paper fasteners are used on the sleeves, pockets and the points of the sides of the coat front, as well as on either side of the front below the turned back lapels. The pockets are attached to the jacket front as shown

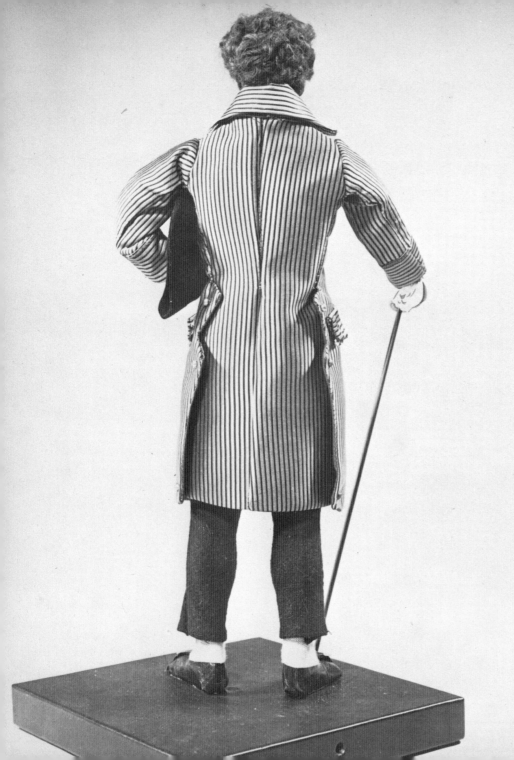

53

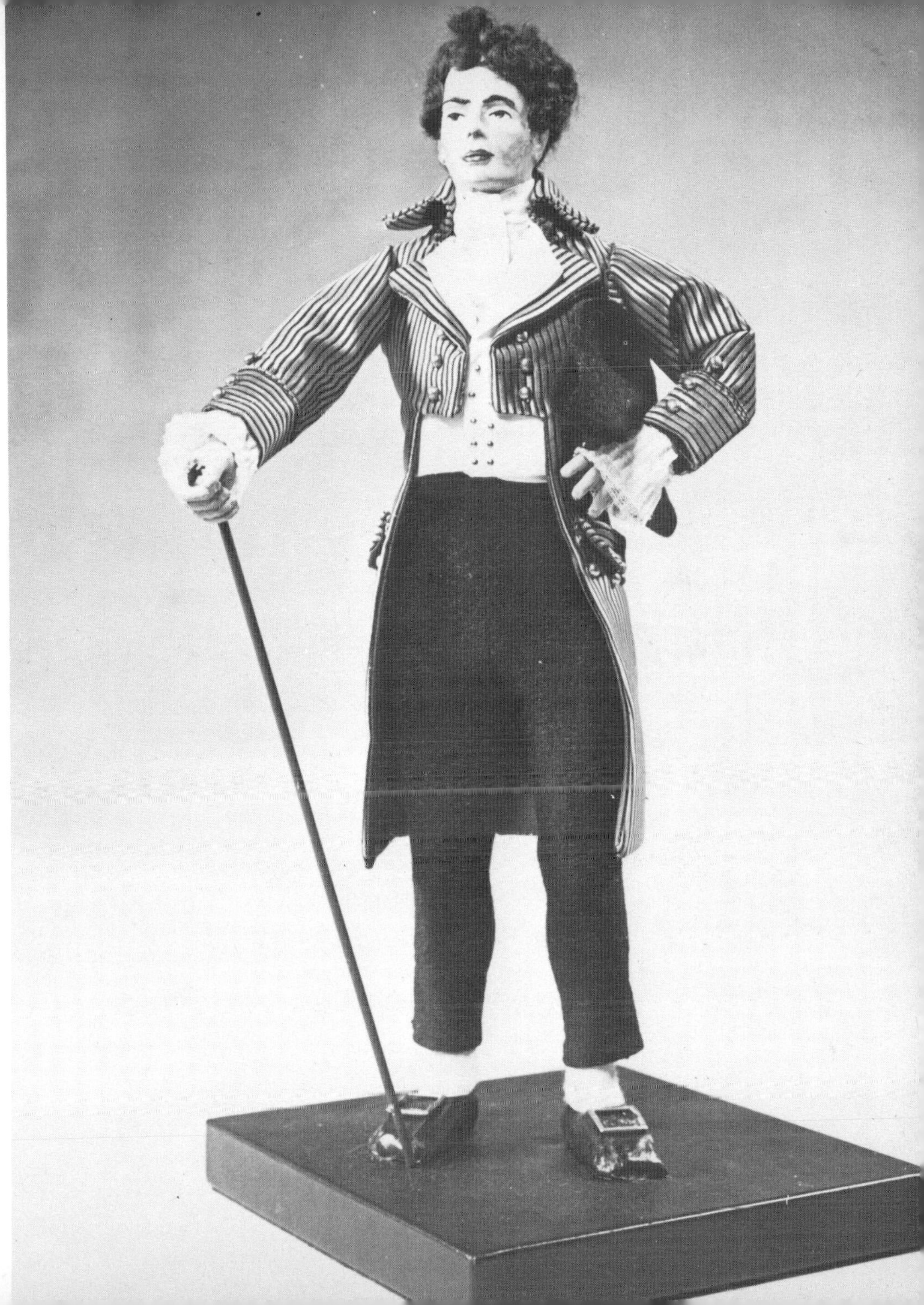

in the diagram. The cuffs are attached to the sleeves which are then sewn to the jacket at the armhole edge, after the shoulder seams have been joined. The collar can then be attached to the neckline. The sleeves can now be sewn up and the sides of the coat joined (C to D), the coat fronts overlapping the back.

Lady of *c.* 1834

The requirements to make this charming doll are as follows:

1 A completed display base (see Fig 21)
2 Two lengths of wire for support
3 Leg castings
4 Two lengths of finger bandaging for the stockings
5 One pair of cut upper shoe shapes and a pair of cardboard soles
6 A stuffed full body
7 Underwear garments
8 A length of wire for the arms
9 Nylon or crepe hair to make the wig
10 The female head and shoulder castings
11 The hand castings
12 The costume accessories

The painting of the head and shoulders, hands and the wigging:

The head, shoulders and hands are painted over in a priming of matt white. After a short wait paint the eye socket area with a blueish white. The iris can now be painted in, this being a circle of either blue or brown. Taking the corners of the mouth as a guide mark in with a fine brush the pupil by a small black dot. Now with a mixture of white and burnt sienna mark out the upper and lower eyelids, cutting the top lid in a slightly arching line, just cutting the top of the iris circle. Place on the palette the following colours: white, yellow and burnt sienna, and mix these thoroughly together until the required flesh tint is ready. Now paint on the flesh colour bringing the colour to the eyes blending the outline of the eye into the flesh colour of the face. While still wet paint under the cheek-bone formation with red, blending this into the flesh mass colour of the face. With the same colour paint in the mouth. Apply a little darker red to the upper lip. Apply a little more burnt sienna to the flesh colour paint, and apply around the eyes, down either side of the nose, under the lower lip and under the chin. Blend this into the face. Allow this to dry thoroughly. With a pure burnt sienna mark out the eye-

brows, the upper eyelid, the nostrils and the separation line between the lips. The hands are treated between the fingers with the same colour as that used around the eyes and nose. Now mark out with pure burnt sienna the separation line of the fingers.

The hair style for this model is a little more difficult to make, so the instructions must be followed very carefully. The hairline is pencilled in across the forehead, down either side of the face, behind the ears down to the nape of the neck. This is smeared with glue. Take a length of hair and glue down either end. Place one end of the hair width-wise from the centre peak towards the back of the head. Press down, taking the end and pull it around the back of the head, pressing firmly down just over the ear, then down to the nape of the neck. Press firmly and securely down. Repeat this operation on the other side. The basic wig is completed. Take three lengths of hair and glue the ends of each one. Now join by turning the ends one to the other, forming loops. The loops are then joined together, fanned out then glued securely in the centre of the head and placed in an upright position. A bow or Spanish type comb can decorate these. Lengths of hair glued and rolled are then cut into even smaller rolls, these being built up on either side of the head representing clusters of curls. This was a popular style of the 1830's. Now set the head aside to dry.

Assembling the doll

Through the holes bored in the completed display base, insert the wire securely; fasten down under the base very firmly with a staple and then cover up with a square of felt. Now cover the leg castings with the finger tube bandaging material, securely at the top and under the foot with glue. Smear with glue the upper foot and the upper shoe shape, and press them firmly together, ensuring that the sides and the heel sections are well stuck. Glue the underside of the foot and the cardboard sole and press them firmly one to the other. When dry the covered leg castings are placed over the

54

wires. The long drawers are fitted over the wires and pulled down over the leg castings. The full soft body is nicked at all extremities and with a spot of glue on the leg stumps the body is placed over the wires, through the openings on the leg stumps, and pulled down until contact with the leg casting is made. The drawers are pulled up until the waistband reaches the waist of the soft body, and then it is securely fastened by sewing them together. The arm wire is pushed through the arm openings and the ends of the wire are turned over with the aid of the long-nosed pliers. The petticoat is now dropped over and sewn on via the waistband onto the soft figure. The dress is now placed over the figure. The completed head is smeared with glue on the inside and placed over the soft body and firmly pressed on (Fig 54). The bodice of the dress is pulled up to the shoulder casting and the back is now sewn up neatly (Fig 55). The ends of the soft body arms are now glued and the arm castings inserted over the wire, through the sleeve until contact is made, then pressed firmly in and allowed to set. The large collar piece is now fitted over the shoulders and sewn neatly at the front (Fig 56). The accessories are now attached where required.

Historical note

The angular fashion of the 1830s was popular both in America and Europe. The bodice which fitted down to the waist was now more heavily seamed and boned, and also lined. The neckline became larger and the armhole seam was now more towards the natural shoulder line. The sleeves became so enormous that support of stiffened lining with whalebone or stuffed pads as supports became necessary underneath. These were known as the 'Leg-of-Mutton' sleeves or 'Gigot' sleeves. They were very full at the top becoming tight towards the wrist in a triangular shape. The wide shoulders of the Mancherons which were worn also gave the shoulders a further added width. The skirt became a little shorter, just to ankle length. There was now less decoration, and materials were used more as accessories, such as the wide collars which

55

81

draped over the shoulders. These were known as 'Fichu-Pelerines'. Jewellery was used much more than in the previous decade as bracelets, brooches, earrings, etc. Also at this period was worn the Ferroniere which was a small ornament hanging in the middle of the forehead, usually suspended by a fine chain from around the top of the head.

Costume

The drawers and petticoat are made as previously described.

This dress is very simply made. The skirt is a straight piece of brocade type material gathered to fit at the waist, and joined to the bodice. The collar is a separate piece and lies over the top of the dress and around the shoulders.

The opening is at the back so as to give a smooth front. The darts on either side of the front of the bodice give a pleasant bust line. The front of the bodice is joined to the back pieces at points C and D to make the armhole. The sleeves are then gathered at the top to fit the armholes and sewn in. Then the sides of the bodice and sleeves can be joined.

The collar is made of three pieces, a wing on each side with the main part between. Each part is separately lined in a contrasting colour, and then the wings are sewn to the collar itself on the outside curve, one each side, from E to F. The finished collar is then laid over the shoulders, and the tips of the wings pinned together at the centre front with a small rosette or other small decoration.

56

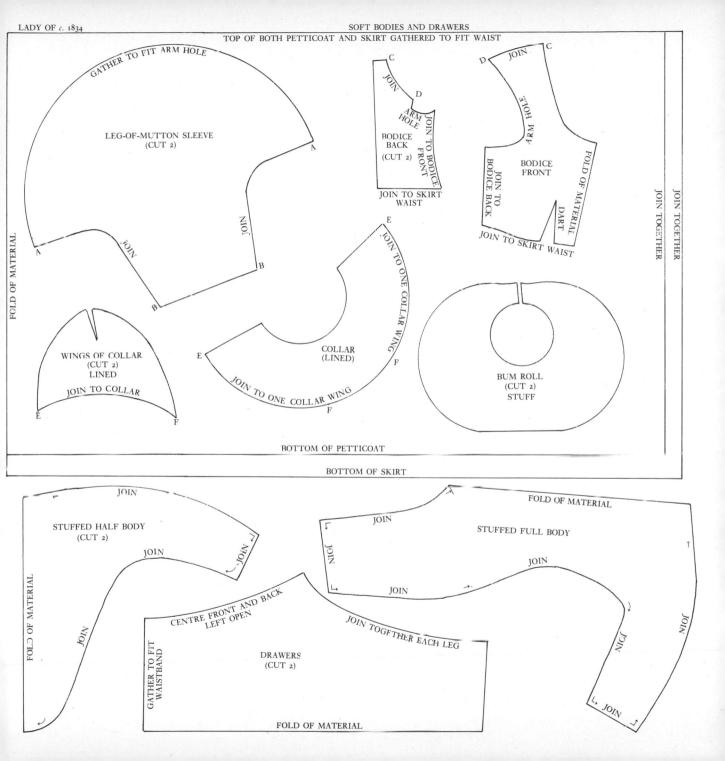

TOP OF BOTH PETTICOAT AND SKIRT GATHERED TO FIT WAIST

GATHER TO FIT ARM HOLE

LEG-OF-MUTTON SLEEVE
(CUT 2)

A

JOIN

JOIN

B

B

FOLD OF MATERIAL

A

JOIN

C

JOIN

D

ARM
HOLE

BODICE
BACK
(CUT 2)

JOIN TO BODICE FRONT

JOIN TO SKIRT
WAIST

D

JOIN

C

ARM HOLE

JOIN TO
BODICE BACK

BODICE
FRONT

FOLD OF MATERIAL

DART

JOIN TO SKIRT WAIST

JOIN TOGETHER

JOIN TOGETHER

E

JOIN TO ONE COLLAR WING

COLLAR
(LINED)

F

E

JOIN TO ONE COLLAR WING

F

WINGS OF COLLAR
(CUT 2)
LINED

JOIN TO COLLAR

E

F

BUM ROLL
(CUT 2)
STUFF

BOTTOM OF PETTICOAT

BOTTOM OF SKIRT

JOIN

STUFFED HALF BODY
(CUT 2)

JOIN

JOIN

FOLD OF MATERIAL

JOIN

JOIN

FOLD OF MATERIAL

JOIN

STUFFED FULL BODY

JOIN

JOIN

JOIN

JOIN

JOIN

CENTRE FRONT AND BACK
LEFT OPEN

JOIN TOGETHER EACH LEG

GATHER TO FIT
WAISTBAND

DRAWERS
(CUT 2)

FOLD OF MATERIAL

58

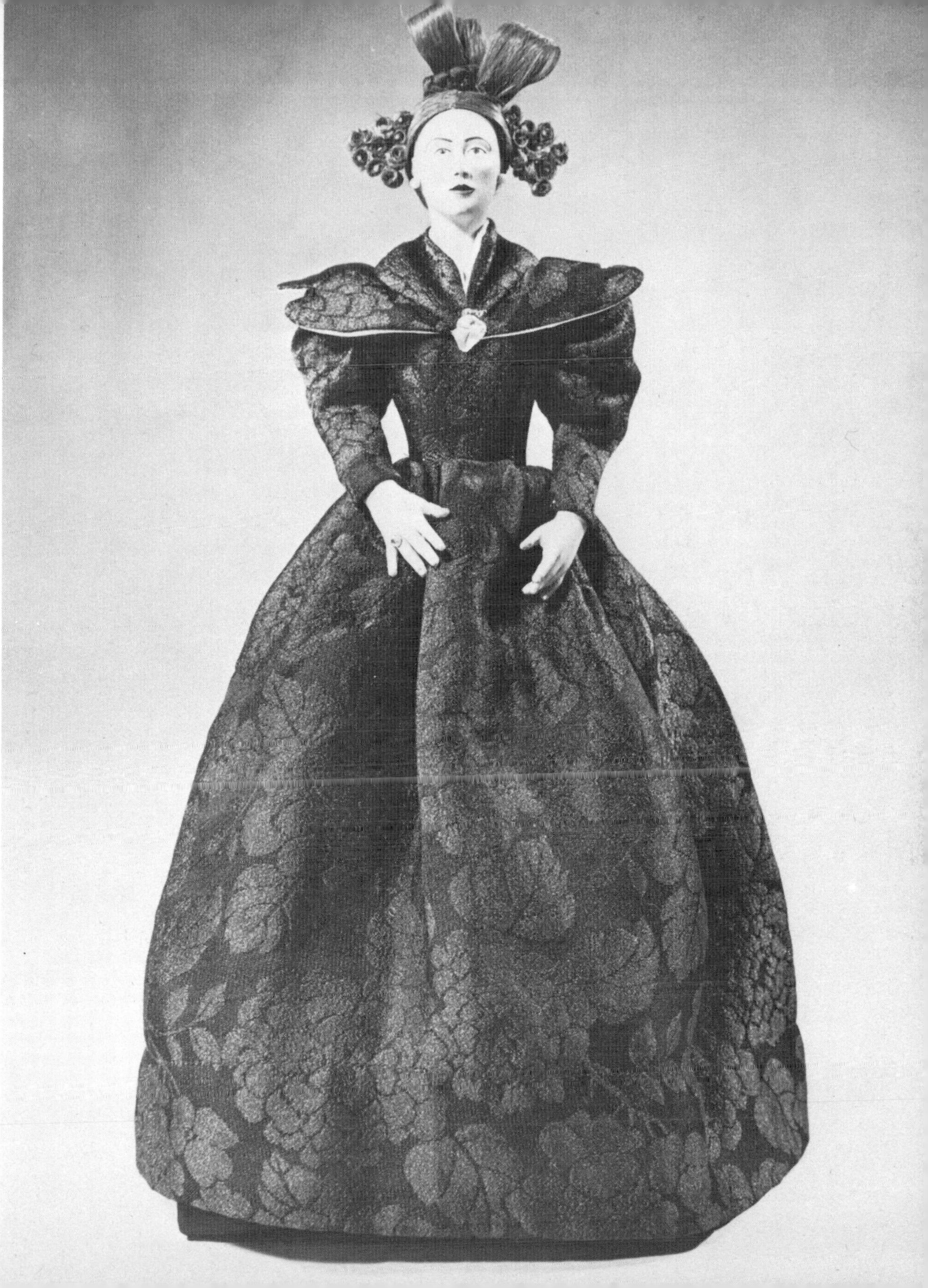

A 'Boston Bustle' Lady *c*. 1885

Requirements for making the bustle fashion doll is as follows:

1   The completed display base
2   The dowel stick centre support with a hole drilled through a third from the top
3   A length of wire for the bustle support
4   A stuffed half body and the horse-shoe shaped bum roll
5   A length of wire for the arm support
6   Matt oil paints
7   Nylon or crepe hair for the wig
8   Head and shoulder casting
9   Petticoat
10 Costume
11 Hand castings
12 The costume accessories

First the painting and wigging of the head and arm castings. Paint both the castings overall in a white matt priming paint. Allow this to dry then over the eye and eyesocket area use the same paint but with just an added touch of blue. The paint recommended is fairly quick drying so the time lag is very short. Now paint on the eyeball itself dead centre a small circle of either blue or brown. This is the iris. Taking the corners of the mouth as a guide place in the centre of the coloured iris a small black dot. This is the pupil. With a mixture of white and burnt sienna mark out very carefully the upper and lower eyelids making the top lid in a slightly arching line just cutting the top of the coloured circle of the iris. Onto a palette place the following colours: burnt sienna, yellow and white. Mix together the burnt sienna and yellow first, this will make a deep flesh tint. Now add the white until the desired flesh tone has been achieved. As this is a lady, a very delicate tinge should be the correct colour. Now apply to the casting, bringing the flesh tone up to and around the eyes blending very carefully the eyelid colour into the flesh tone. Now mix on the palette a spot of red with the flesh colour into a faint shade of pink, and whilst the flesh is still wet, apply a touch of the pink to just under the cheek-bone formation and blend in.

With the flesh tone still in its wet condition, mix with the original flesh colour a small quantity of burnt sienna. Mix thoroughly and then apply around the eyes, down either side of the nose, under the bottom lip and under the chin, blending this into the neck. The mouth should be painted in the same pink colour and the upper lip touched in with a deeper pink or red. Now with a pure burnt sienna colour mark in the upper eyelids, the nostrils, and the separation line of the lips. The hand and arm casting must also be painted overall in the flesh colour. In between the fingers apply the deeper tone colour used around the eyes and nose. Knuckles and joints can be touched with the pink colour, and also with a pure burnt sienna line between the fingers. With the head casting thoroughly dry, mark with a fine pencil line the hairline across the forehead, down either side of the face, over the ears, then down the back of the head to the nape of the neck. Glue over the area enclosed in the pencilled outline, cut three lengths of hair long enough to cover the head and hang half-way down the back. Glue both ends of these strips and with the hair hanging over the face of the doll, press the edge of the strip firmly onto the hairline of the forehead. Repeat this operation on either side of the face, pressing very firmly down. Place a padding, which can be a roll of paper, over the front of the head, this will give the hair the added height required for this hair style. Now, bring each strip length in turn starting from the centre and turn it back on itself and over the head pressing it down onto the head leaving the ends hanging down the back. Having turned the three lengths back, take them together and make a loop, turning them back and secure on the crown of the head with a short length of cotton. This can be covered later by a broader piece of ribbon. This may now be set aside until the final assembly.

Assembling the doll

Into the centre hole of the completed display base fit the dowel stick, which is the centre support. Through the small hole which is drilled through the dowel stick insert a length of

59

60

wire and form a loop then fasten off by winding the ends of wire onto the stick. Sew onto this wire loop the horse-shoe shaped bum roll (Fig 59). Nick the half-body at the centre neck at the base and at either arm piece. A length of wire is now pushed through these arm openings and the protruding ends are turned back with the long nosed pliers. Slide the soft body over the dowel stick, now put over the petticoat and sew the waistband to the stuffed body (Fig 60). The skirt

61   62

part is now fitted over the stick and arranged over the bustle
formation, sewn onto the petticoat waistband and attached to
the soft body to make it secure (Fig 61). The bodice piece is
now put on and pulled down. The head and shoulder casting
is smeared on the inside with glue and pressed firmly onto the
soft body. The bodice is pulled up and fitted over the shoulders
of the casting and fashioned to the body, and the back opening
is sewn up neatly. A touch of glue is applied to the soft body

89

arm pieces and the arm and hand castings are inserted through the sleeves over the wire until contact is made with the soft arm stumps and then pressed firmly together and allowed to set (Fig 62). The accessories can now be added to complete the bustle fashion doll.

Historical note

The most conspicuous outline for the lady of fashion in the decade of 1880 to 1890 was the enormous bustle. Although the bustle itself had a period of about the middle of the 1860's when the crinoline was going out of fashion and the fullness of the skirt material without the hoops was being drawn up at the sides like paniers and then pushed backwards, this style became unfashionable about 1870. Then came slowly back with the aid of mechanical devices, like the *cage Américaine*, manufactured from bone or wire and returned to the peak of fashion between 1885 and 1890, when it reached its maximum dimensions, being projected backwards like a ledge. The mechanical contrivances, being made from the steel or bone hoops, caused the protuberance to swing from side to side in a most unnatural swaying movement. The bustle itself was achieved in various ways, some as stuffed cushions sewn into the back of the skirt and supported by the steel hoops, sewn in a fixed horizontal position into the lining, then put into shape with back tapes thus pulling the front flat and making the back skirt project. The wasp waist was tight and rigid and with the bustle all natural contours of the body were completely concealed giving, as always, for the lady of fashion an appearance of great unnaturalness. The sleeve-style of this period formed a large unusual large puff at the shoulder then descended to a tight sleeve at the wrist. The hair style adopted was the chignon which was made as large as possible, the hair being brushed away from the face, often with wispy fringes over the forehead. A wire cage was often placed on the head and masses of hair was piled onto it, the coiffure being decorated with trimmings of lace or ribbon. The hat had now almost taken over the place of the bonnet and was quite small

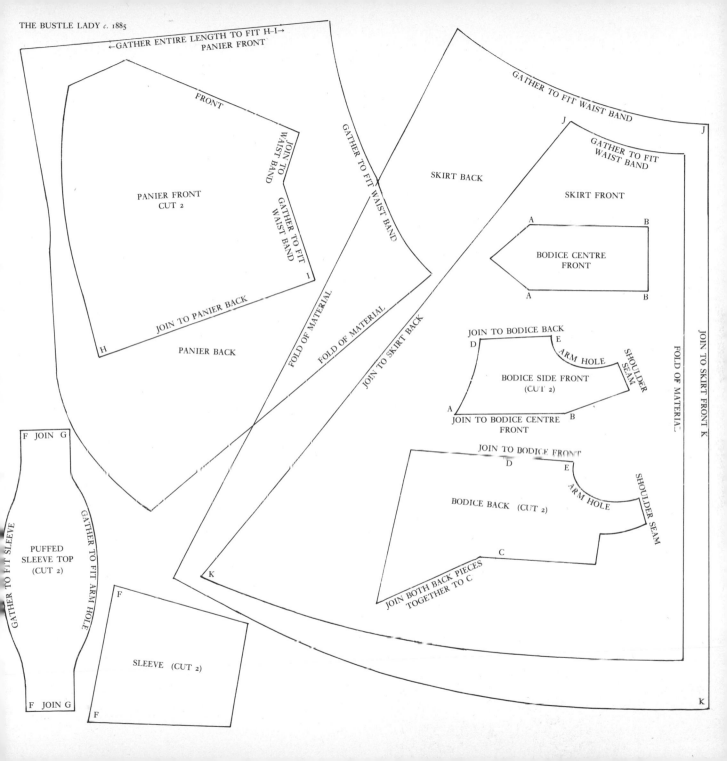

THE BUSTLE LADY *c.* 1885

←GATHER ENTIRE LENGTH TO FIT H-I→
PANIER FRONT

FRONT

JOIN TO WAIST BAND

GATHER TO FIT WAIST BAND

PANIER FRONT
CUT 2

I

GATHER TO FIT WAIST BAND

FOLD OF MATERIAL

FOLD OF MATERIAL

SKIRT BACK

GATHER TO FIT WAIST BAND

J

GATHER TO FIT WAIST BAND

J

SKIRT FRONT

A   B

BODICE CENTRE
FRONT

A   B

JOIN TO PANIER BACK

H

PANIER BACK

JOIN TO SKIRT BACK

JOIN TO BODICE BACK

D   E

ARM HOLE

SHOULDER SEAM

BODICE SIDE FRONT
(CUT 2)

A   B

JOIN TO BODICE CENTRE
FRONT

FOLD OF MATERIAL

JOIN TO SKIRT FRONT K

JOIN TO BODICE FRONT

D   E

ARM HOLE

SHOULDER SEAM

BODICE BACK   (CUT 2)

C

JOIN BOTH BACK PIECES
TOGETHER TO C

F JOIN G

GATHER TO FIT SLEEVE

PUFFED
SLEEVE TOP
(CUT 2)

GATHER TO FIT ARM HOLE

F JOIN G

K

F

F

SLEEVE   (CUT 2)

F

K

64

and worn perched forward on the forehead with the heavy coiffure massed at the back, not unlike the bustle itself, often being trimmed with lace, ribbon, flowers and veils, and more often than not, brimless. The shoes had round toes and low heels with lace-up fronts usually made from kid. The stockings were made from cotton, cashmere or silk and in almost every colour shade. Fans were often carried and were usually large of the ostrich feather type.

Costume

To make this dress is not as complicated or difficult as it may seem at first glance.

The skirt is made of two pieces of material, gathered to a waistband, the longer part hanging towards the back, with the bum roll beneath. The paniers are made of three parts, the back part of the panier is gathered at the sides to fit the sides of the fronts, and then attached to a waistband, but leaving a slight gap open at the centre front. The paniers are edged all round in a contrasting narrow braid, which can be slightly scallopped.

The bodice is also edged in braid at the neckline and around the bottom edge. It is made of several parts. The sleeves are also made in two pieces – the puffed top half is joined to the fitted part, the puff being gathered to fit the top of the fitted bottom part at F, and the top of the puffed sleeve at G, gathered to fit the armhole of the bodice when the shoulder seams have been joined together. The back of the bodice is left open from the neckline to C at waist level to fit over the model, and is then either sewn or pinned together.

Glossary

Alb A long-sleeved embroidered garment reaching to the ground.

Amice A white linen rectangular piece of material, like a collar, tied over the chest and neck with string.

Baldric A belt or sash hung from one shoulder to the opposite hip to carry a sword or other object. Was also often worn around the waist.

Bicorne A hat with two points, one towards the front and the other to the back.

Bombast A type of cotton padding.

Breeches A type of trouser.

Buckram A coarse material stiffened with glue.

Bum Roll A stuffed piece of material, sausage shaped, placed around the body to push the skirt out, giving a bustle-like appearance.

Bustle Originally a kind of crinoline, the skirt wider at the back and standing away supported by a bum roll or padded cushion.

Camisole An under-bodice.

Canions Under-breeches which appeared as short tube-like additions to the bottom of the puffed-out trunk-hose, reaching to the knees.

Cassock A straight long garment with a standing collar worn under the alb.

Cope A cape or cloak worn over the alb, made of a semi-circular piece of material open down the front and fastened over the chest with a band.

Cravat A tie or neckcloth.

Crinoline A stiff petticoat, originally made of crin or horsehair, a wide skirt standing away from the body in a conical shape.

Crosier A staff in the shape of a shepherd's crook.

Doublet A padded short jacket, well fitting.

Farthingale A hooped skirt stiffened with horsehair or canvas, usually on hoops of cane, whalebones or wire.

Ferroniere A fine chain around the head with just a single precious stone suspended over the centre of the forehead.

Fichu-pelerine A cape or collar draped around the neck and shoulders, made of a very fine material.

Flash A seepage of latex composition or liquid through the mould joins.

Gigot sleeves Also known as leg-of-mutton sleeves. Fully puffed at the top, but tight fitting from the elbow down.

Hanging sleeves A false sleeve, part of the outer garment, just sewn together at the top.

Mancherons A wide collar or flounced epaulettes.

Mitre Hat A tall cap with triangular up standing pieces.

Orphrey Gold embroidered band applied to the cope and base of the alb.

Palisadoes Wire supports to raise the hair at the front.

Paniers Hoops usually made of wicker, worn on either side of the waist or at the back.

Cote-hardie A medieval fashion garment worn by both male and female. A low-necked tight fitting gown, being buttoned down the front to the waist with a full skirt below the knees. Later became tunic length for the male.

Frontlet Usually a velvet or embroidered length of material which covered the forehead when wearing a hennin.

Hennin Lady's head gear which was a tall pointed steeple shaped headdress. The origin is unknown, but it is usually referred to as a Flemish fashion.

Houppelande An overgarment later called a gown. Worn by both male and female. Close fitting to the waist and fell in long folds to the ground. The sleeves were funnel shaped with wide cuffs and were often long to the ground.

Kirtle   A name given to the female version of the male fashion which was a long tight fitting gown with long close fitting sleeves, usually worn with a belt around the hips.

Surcoat   A sideless garment consisting of two pieces, a front and a back, attached at the shoulders and being fastened around the hips with a belt of material.

Pantaloons   Long tight trousers, opening at the front in a panel shape.

Pomander   A small ball-shaped holder containing musk or any scent or perfume.

Registration keys   Impressions and protrusions opposite each other, allowing the moulds to be placed accurately together.

Roll or shawl collar   A long collar without a point.

Rose   A rosette worn on the instep of a shoe.

Rosette   A rose shape made of pleated ribbon or ribbon loops.

Ruff   A wide collar made to stand up by being starched and folded and supported by wires.

Stand-fall collar   A high standing collar turned over, falling down with a deep fold.

Steinkirk   A kind of cravat or scarf tied loosely.

Stomacher   A decorative false front ending in a point.

Trunk hose   Puffed out short breeches which were part of the stockings.

Whalebone   A pliable horny substance used as stiffening.

Where to get materials

Art and Craft Shops
Draughtsmans dividers, Metal spatulas, Paint brushes, Pallette, Plasticine, Wire-ended tools, Wooden spatulas.

Bellman, Ivey & Carter Ltd
358–374, Grand Drive, Raynes Park, S.W.20
Latex composition, Plaster of paris.

Chemist
Finger bandaging

Departmental Stores
Copydex, Dog studs, Kapok, Large headed pins, Nylon hair, Paper fasteners

D.I.Y. or Hardware Shops
Galvanised wire, Plaster of paris, Rubber-based adhesive i.e. Evostick or Copydex, Wood for modelling board and bases, Wooden dowelling, Sandpaper

Model Shop
Matt oil paints i.e. Humbrol or Airfix, Paint brushes